Lucky Santangelo Novels
by Jackie Collins

Goddess of Vengeance
Drop Dead Beautiful
Dangerous Kiss
Vendetta: Lucky's Revenge
Lady Boss
Lucky
Chances

Also by Jackie Collins

The Power Trip
Poor Little Bitch Girl
Married Lovers
Lovers & Players
Hollywood Divorces
Deadly Embrace
Hollywood Wives—The New Generation
Lethal Seduction
L.A. Connections: Power, Obsession, Murder, Revenge
Thrill!
Hollywood Kids
American Star
Rock Star
Hollywood Husbands
Lovers and Gamblers
Hollywood Wives
The World Is Full of Divorced Women
The Love Killers
Sinners
The Bitch
The Stud
The World Is Full of Married Men

The Lucky Santangelo Cookbook

JACKIE COLLINS

ST. MARTIN'S PRESS ☵ NEW YORK

THE LUCKY SANTANGELO COOKBOOK. Copyright © 2014 by Chances, Inc. All rights reserved. Printed in China. For information, address St. Martin's Press, 175 Fifth Avenue, New York, N.Y. 10010.

Food Photography by Amy Roth
Additional photos by Eddie Sanderson
Illustrations by Michelle Beilner
Recipe Testing and Development by Tom Steele

Designed by James Sinclair

www.stmartins.com

Library of Congress Cataloging-in-Publication Data

Collins, Jackie.
  The Lucky Santangelo cookbook / Jackie Collins. — First U.S. Edition.
     pages cm
   ISBN 978-1-250-01465-8 (hardcover)
   ISBN 978-1-4668-4271-7 (e-book)
1. Italian American women—Fiction. 2. Cooking—Fiction. 3. Cookbooks—Fiction. 4. Entertaining—Fiction. 5. Dinners and dining—Fiction. 6. Domestic fiction. I. Title.
  PR6053.O425L84 2014
  823'.914—dc23
                    2013031863

St. Martin's Press books may be purchased for educational, business, or promotional use. For information on bulk purchases, please contact Macmillan Corporate and Premium Sales Department at 1-800-221-7945, extension 5442, or write specialmarkets@macmillan.com.

First Edition: April 2014

10   9   8   7   6   5   4   3   2   1

To all you foodies out there, eat & be LUCKY!!!

Contents

Introduction 1

About Jackie Collins 2

About Lucky Santangelo 3

Cocktails

The Jackie Collins, by Wolfgang Puck 7

The Venus Bellini 8

Caipirinhas 10

Lucky's Killer Margaritas 11

Lennie Has a Yen for the Definitive Manhattan 12

Gino the Ram's Special Spicy Bloody Marys 13

Bobby and Denver's White Wine Sangria 14

Wassail 15

Midori Sours 15

The Venus Lychee Martini 16

Appetizers

Amazing Caesar Salad 20

Max's Beet and Avocado Salad 23

Mandarin Orange and Red Onion Salad
with Champagne 25

Chorizo-Chocolate Tapas 26

Mushroom and Gruyère Tart 28

Creamy Macaroni and Cheese 29

Smoked Duck Pizza with Hoisin Sauce 30

Pizza with Mushroom and Sausage 31

Gino's Favorite Pesto Pizza 33

Smoked Salmon Pizza 34

Pasta Appetizers

Lemon Linguine 38

Rigatoni with Bacon and Shiitake Mushrooms 39

Penne alla Vodka Martini with Tomato,
Sausage, Bacon, and Cream 40

Pasta Puttanesca 42

Angel Hair Pasta with Sweet Sausage,
Saffron, and Cream 43

Lasagne with Wild Mushrooms, Sausage,
Four Cheeses, and Prosciutto 44

Veal Saffron Cream Pasta Sauce 46

Fettuccine with Crab and Cream 47

Fettuccine with Clams and Chorizo 48

Rigatoni with Lobster Champagne Cream 50

Entrées

Zucchini Boats   55

Eggplant Parmesan   56

Deviled Chicken Drumsticks   57

Lucky's Special Southern Fried Chicken   58

Chicken Breasts with Fontina and Prosciutto   59

Chicken Paella with Spanish Chorizo   60

Chicken Cacciatore   62

Bourbon Chicken Milanese   63

Grilled Lime Chicken with Fontina Cheese and
   Dried Chile Sauce   64

Chicken Breasts with Roasted Lemon, Green Olive,
   and Capers   67

Coq au Vin   68

Roasted Sage Sausages and Grapes   70

Duck Burgers with Onion Marmalade   71

Lucky's Get-You-Going Turkey   72

Pork Chops Milanese   73

Pork Chops Saltimbocca with Sautéed Spinach   74

Pork Tenderloin with Honey-Mustard Sauce   75

Pulled Pork Tacos   77

Sweet and Spicy Spareribs   78

Lucky's Luscious Meatballs   80

The Best Hamburger in Town!   83

Peppered Beef Stroganoff   84

Lucky's Kick-Ass Chili   86

Rococo Meat loaf   88

Beef Tenderloin Steaks with Brandy and
   Mustard Sauce   90

Steak Tartare   91

Roast Beef Dusted with Coriander   93

Bourbon-Marinated Flank Steak   94

Lamb Steaks with Mushrooms   95

Lamb You Can Eat with a Spoon   96

Roasted Veal Scallops with Vegetables   97

Shrimp in Lemony Coconut Milk   98

Santangelo Salmon   101

Skate with Lobster Rice   102

Sole with Parmesan Crust   103

Delicious Side Dishes

New Potato Salad   106

Potato Balls Sautéed in Butter   107

The Best Mashed Potatoes Ever!   108

English Roast Potatoes   109

Roasted Butternut Squash   110

Sweet Potatoes and Apricots   111

Creamy Peas with Tarragon   112

Green Beans with Cumin for a Crowd   113

Slow-Braised Green Beans   114

Creamed Fresh Corn–Stuffed
   Red Bell Peppers   115

Roasted Broccoli with Fondue   118

Brussels Sprouts Moutarde   121

Cheesy Cauliflower Gratin   123

Blue Cheese and Caramelized
   Onion Potatoes au Gratin   124

Crabby Portobello Mushrooms   125

Incredible Sauces

Cranberry-Orange Chutney   128

Plum Glaze   129

Barbecue "Gonzalez" Sauce   129

Lucky's Best Besciamella Sauce   130

Blender Hollandaise Sauce   131

Delectable Desserts

Baked Peaches with Cointreau   135

Pear Tart   136

Apple Crumble   137

Pear and Blueberry Pie with Buttery
   Oatmeal Crust   138

Perfect Cherry Pie   139

Butterscotch Pie   140

Moist Sugar Cake   141

Rich Carrot Cake   142

To-Die-For Cheesecake   143

Crème Brûlée   145

Flourless Chocolate Cake   147

Molten Chocolate Tarts   148

Intense Lemon Sorbet   149

Crème Fraîche with Chocolate Mousse   151

Buttermilk Panna Cotta with Strawberries   152

Coconut Sorbet   154

Index   157

The

Lucky Santangelo

Cookbook

Introduction

Hey everyone. You've all been asking for it, and finally here it is—*The Lucky Santangelo Cookbook*, featuring all of Lucky's favorite recipes (and many of mine!).

I've had a fantastic time writing seven books about Lucky and the Santangelo family, and now to share her cooking skills with you is a real treat, for Lucky loves a family cookout. From delish meatballs to sweet and spicy spareribs (a Bobby and Max favorite), Lucky—as in everything else—excels in the kitchen. Big family dinners are her forte. She likes nothing better than having everyone sitting around her table, ready and waiting to sample her cooking talents.

For a true family event there will be her irascible dad, Gino Santangelo—a man still going strong in his nineties, and his current wife, Paige (there have been several!). Then there's Lucky's husband, Lennie, the very laid-back and attractive writer/director/producer. And of course Bobby Santangelo Stanislopoulos, Lucky's extraordinarily handsome and charming twentysomething son, along with his very smart girlfriend, Deputy DA Denver Jones. And let us not forget Max, Lucky's wild teenage daughter, a girl just like her mom—maybe even wilder! And Max's younger brother, Gino Junior, plus Leonardo (Lennie's son from a long-ago one-night indiscretion). Oh, yes, and if Lucky's half-brother Steven is in town, he'll be there, too—with his supermodel wife, Lina, and teenage daughter, Carioca.

Friends always drop by at family events: Lucky's closest friend, blonde superstar, Venus, with her boy toy of the moment; Lucky's trusty personal assistant, Danny, along with his partner, Buff; and the famous movie director Alex Stone, one of Lucky's most ardent admirers. (Usually Alex will be accompanied by his latest date—often an exquisite Asian woman.)

The Santangelo family enjoy nothing better than getting together for a fabulous feast. So . . . join the Santangelo clan, and most of all eat well and have fun!

Bon appétit!

About Jackie Collins

With more than 500 million copies of her thirty bestselling novels sold around the world, countless national television appearances, an illustrious writing career, and access to some of the most famous people on the planet, Jackie Collins certainly needs no introduction. From Beverly Hills bedrooms to raunchy prowls along the shadowy streets of Hollywood; from glittering rock concerts and parties to stretch limos with wet bars and the mansions of ravenous power brokers—Collins chronicles the real truth from the inside looking out. The late director Louis Malle called Collins "a raunchy moralist," and *Vanity Fair* magazine referred to her as "Hollywood's own Marcel Proust." She isn't afraid to give her readers a true insider's knowledge of the glamorous lives and loves of the rich, famous, and infamous. "I write about real people in disguise," she has said. "If anything, my characters are toned down—the truth is much more bizarre."

Jackie has always been an avid cook, and loves all kinds of food, especially Italian dishes, and especially Lucky's homegrown recipes.

One of Jackie's favorite characters to write about has always been the wild and wonderful Lucky Santangelo. "Lucky inspires women to be stronger," Jackie says. "She is a positive role model with a true kick-ass attitude. I love writing her. And my readers respond to her in a big and very positive way. She is a true female superhero. I have now written seven books about the Santangelo family, and I hope to write many more as Lucky and Lennie's families grow and evolve.

A special favorite character is Lucky's charismatic son, Bobby. He has so many adventures ahead of him, so keep reading! And Max, Lennie and Lucky's teenage daughter. Max is a wild one, just like her mom—so watch out!"

About Lucky Santangelo

Bold, wildly beautiful, and totally her own woman, Lucky Santangelo needs no introduction. The sizzling, glamorous, sometimes dangerous daughter of former gangster Gino, Lucky is the most popular character in Collins's wild world of lust, intrigue, violence, and redemption. Lucky is central to seven of Collins's wildly popular novels: *Chances, Lucky, Lady Boss, Vendetta: Lucky's Revenge, Dangerous Kiss, Drop Dead Beautiful,* and *Goddess of Vengeance.* Lucky ruled in two extremely successful NBC Television miniseries—*Lucky Chances* starring Nicollette Sheridan as Lucky and Sandra Bullock as her nineteen-year-old mom, and then *Lady Boss* starring Kim Delaney as Lucky.

Everyone loved watching Lucky come to life; she strode across the screen like a beautiful and powerful James Bond for women. Readers and viewers alike adore Lucky because she says and does all the things they would really like to say and do, but don't quite have the stones to do so!

And Lucky takes care of her family. A true Italian-American woman of the world, she still likes to shake it up in the kitchen. From traditional Italian dishes to sumptuous desserts and crazy cocktails, Lucky puts it all together.

So . . . if you want a little taste of Lucky Santangelo in your life . . . get into the kitchen and start getting Lucky!

Cocktails

The Jackie Collins, by Wolfgang Puck

The Venus Bellini

Caipirinhas

Lucky's Killer Margaritas

Lennie Has a Yen for the Definitive Manhattan

Gino the Ram's Special Spicy Bloody Marys

Bobby and Denver's White Wine Sangria

Wassail

Midori Sours

The Venus Lychee Martini

The Jackie Collins, by Wolfgang Puck

Yield: 1 Jackie Collins cocktail

Muddle the raspberries with the simple syrup. Add the vodka and lemonade into a cocktail shaker. Squeeze the lime over the vodka mixture. Add the ice cubes, and shake the cocktail shaker hard for 30 seconds. Pour in the club soda, shake once, and strain into a highball glass. Garnish with a raspberry and a fresh mint leaf.

6 raspberries plus an additional raspberry, for garnish

Splash of simple syrup (1 ounce or less)

2 ounces vodka

2 ounces lemonade, preferably Perricone's

½ lime

4 to 6 ice cubes

1½ ounces club soda

Fresh mint leaf, for garnish

Jackie with Wolf and Mark Steines.

What can I say about Wolf except that he's the BEST! I have never had anything but exquisite meals at all of his many restaurants. And when he created The Jackie Collins I was totally thrilled. Thank you, Wolf, and keep on doing it so brilliantly! Oh, and yes everyone, enjoy the drink!

The Venus Bellini

Yield: about 6 Bellinis

Frozen passion fruit purée is becoming much more widely available in city supermarkets—great news for Lucky's fantastic Bellinis.

½ cup filtered water

1 cup superfine sugar

8 ounces frozen sliced peaches, thawed

1 teaspoon grated tangerine peel

8 ounces frozen strawberries, thawed

8 ounces frozen passion fruit purée, thawed

3 to 4 bottles good-quality champagne, or prosecco, chilled

Fresh strawberries, for garnish

Orange and lemon peel twists, for garnish

In a medium saucepan over medium heat, heat the water and sugar and stir steadily until the sugar has dissolved, 4 to 5 minutes. Set the sugar syrup aside to let cool.

In the jar of a blender, purée the peaches, tangerine peel, and ¼ cup of the sugar syrup until very smooth. Strain into a medium bowl, cover with plastic wrap, and refrigerate.

What a way to start any evening—or finish it for that matter—an ice cold Bellini or The Jackie Collins by Wolfgang Puck is always a delight!

Drink up and have fun.

Clean the blender jar, add the strawberries and ¼ cup of the sugar syrup and purée until smooth. Strain into another bowl through a fine-mesh strainer or a strainer lined with cheesecloth, and discard the strawberry seeds. Cover the bowl with plastic wrap and refrigerate.

Clean the blender jar again, add the passion fruit purée and purée with the remaining sugar syrup until smooth. Pour into a small pitcher, and transfer the chilled strawberry and peach mixtures into two other small pitchers.

For each Bellini, have your guests choose their preferred fruit mixture and pour about 3 tablespoons of the chosen mixture into a tall champagne flute. Slowly pour enough champagne or prosecco into the flute until it's filled. Garnish with the strawberries and orange and lemon twists and serve at once.

Sometimes only a Bellini fixes all the wrongs in the world, Lucky thought as she and her best friend, Venus, indulged their passion. Venus was going through a period of boy toys—young studs in their early twenties with rock-hard abs and a penchant for endless sex. Lucky could only watch and admire Venus's stamina. Who needed a young stud when you are married to Lennie Golden? As far as Lucky was concerned—one of the most attractive and talented men ever.

"Hmm . . ." Venus murmured, sipping her Bellini. "Delicious!"

"The drink or your latest acquisition?" Lucky inquired.

Venus giggled. "He's got abs of steel. I want you to meet him."

"Can't wait," Lucky drawled.

But of course she could.

Caipirinhas

Yield: eight 6-ounce Caipirinhas

These zippy Brazilian libations are smooth and mild in flavor, but they can really sneak up on you!

4 limes, plus 2 additional limes for garnish

2 tablespoons superfine sugar

1 dozen ice cubes

1½ cups cachaça (Brazilian sugarcane liquor)

Quarter all the limes lengthwise, then cut each quarter in half crosswise and place the quarters of 4 of the limes in a pitcher. Add 2 tablespoons of the sugar to the pitcher, then muddle the lime quarters by pounding and pressing with a wooden spoon until the sugar has dissolved. Fill 6 to 8 glasses with ice, add 3 tablespoons (1½ ounces) of cachaça, and stir in the muddled lime mixture to fill each glass.

Cachaça is becoming much more widely available, but you can substitute vodka. They just won't be real Caipirinhas. Use superfine sugar, which is sold in most supermarkets, because it dissolves quickly and thoroughly.

"Hey," Lucky said. "Want a drink?"

Her husband, Lennie, gave her his irresistible lopsided grin. "Only if you feel like making one of your famous Caipirinhas."

"And if I do, what do I get in return?" Lucky challenged.

Lennie's grin widened. "Whatever you want, Lucky. And I got a hunch I know what that might be."

Lucky smiled. "Ah, he knows me so well," she sighed.

"Sure I do," Lennie said confidently.

"And what if what she wants is the latest model Ferrari?"

"For one drink?" Lennie said, raising his eyebrows. "You gotta be—"

"Trust me," Lucky said, lightly running her fingers through his longish hair. "It'll be worth it."

Lennie grinned. He knew it would be. Of that he had no doubt.

Lucky's Killer Margaritas

Yield: 4 to 6 Margaritas

The longer the zest and juice mixture steeps, the better. Twenty-four hours would be ideal. But if you're in a hurry—and when it comes to margaritas, most people are—just omit the zest and skip the steeping process.

Combine the lime zest and juice, lemon zest and juice, grapefruit juice, sugar, and salt in a 1-quart glass measuring cup. Cover with plastic wrap and refrigerate until the flavors blend, 4 to 24 hours.

Divide 1 cup crushed ice among 4 to 6 roomy tumblers, rimmed with salt if desired. Strain the juice mixture into a 1-quart pitcher or cocktail shaker. Add the tequila, Triple Sec, and the remaining cup of crushed ice. Stir or shake until thoroughly combined and chilled, 20 to 60 seconds. Strain into the ice-filled tumblers. Serve immediately.

4 teaspoons finely grated zest, plus ½ cup juice from 2 to 3 medium limes

4 teaspoons finely grated zest, plus ½ cup juice from 2 to 3 medium lemons

⅓ cup freshly squeezed white grapefruit juice

¼ cup superfine sugar

Pinch of salt, plus additional salt for rimming the glasses (optional)

2 cups roughly crushed ice

1½ cups 100 percent agave tequila

1 cup Triple Sec

Lucky is very into all types of music, as am I. When drinking one of Lucky's Killer Margaritas, I suggest you listen to a couple of her favorite tracks, such as "Hero" by Enrique Iglesias and Marvin Gaye's "What's Going On." Have fun with the drink *and* the music.

Lennie Has a Yen for the Definitive Manhattan

Yield: 2 generous Manhattans

When it comes to a Manhattan cocktail, less is always more. There are some dreadful "variations" out there. Perfection should be left alone!

1½ ounces sweet vermouth

5 to 6 ounces good bourbon

2 dashes of Angostura Bitters

2 maraschino cherries

Chilled cocktail glasses, or, preferably, conical stemmed martini glasses

Combine the vermouth, bourbon, and bitters with 7 ice cubes in a cocktail shaker. Shake vigorously to combine.

Place a cherry in each of two chilled cocktail or martini glasses and strain the bourbon mixture over the cherry.

Lennie Golden. A true talent. A director, writer, producer. A man happy and satisfied with his life. And why wouldn't he be? For Lennie is married to the very volatile and vibrant Lucky Santangelo. A one-of-a-kind woman.

Lennie often recalls their first meeting so many years ago in Las Vegas. She'd wanted to sleep with him. He'd turned her down!

Crazy times. Crazy memories.

And now . . . married with kids.

He wouldn't have it any other way.

Gino the Ram's Special Spicy Bloody Marys

Yield: 6 to 8 Bloody Marys

Not for sissies! If you've got a few timid souls in attendance at your soirée, I suppose you could omit the habañero or Scotch bonnet, but it won't be the same experience. If you had to, you could also substitute bottled prepared horseradish for the freshly grated, but again, it won't be the same.

In a 1-quart glass measure, combine the vodka with the onion, pressed garlic, jalapeños, habañero, bell pepper, lemon juice, and hot sauce. Using an immersion blender, purée the mixture until smooth.

In a large pitcher (at least ½-gallon capacity), combine the vodka mixture with the tomato juice, grated horseradish, celery salt, and black pepper and stir vigorously to blend. Strain into ice-filled tall glasses and serve with the lime wedges and celery ribs.

When dealing with Gino—anything goes! The man is a powerhouse, a force of nature.
Drink Gino the Ram's Special Spicy Bloody Mary only if you enjoy taking chances! Good luck!

2½ cups chilled vodka

½ cup chopped onion

2 small garlic cloves, pressed with a sturdy garlic press

2 small jalapeños, stemmed, seeded, and coarsely chopped

1 habañero or Scotch bonnet pepper, stemmed, seeded, and coarsely chopped

1 medium red bell pepper, stemmed, seeded, and coarsely chopped

2 tablespoons freshly squeezed lemon juice

Hot sauce, to taste

5 cups tomato or V8 juice

3 tablespoons peeled and grated fresh horseradish

2 teaspoons celery salt

1 teaspoon freshly ground black pepper

Lime wedges and celery ribs, for serving

Bobby and Denver's White Wine Sangria

Yield: 4 to 6 servings

One 25-ounce bottle white wine (more or less is okay), such as Riesling, Gewürtztraminer, or Chardonnay

½ cup superfine sugar

3 oranges, scrubbed and sliced into wedges

1 lemon, scrubbed and sliced into wedges

1 lime, scrubbed and sliced into wedges

4 ounces brandy

2 cups club soda

You can take this recipe further by adding your favorite fruits— apple and/or pear slices, peeled and sliced kiwi, sliced peaches, sliced strawberries, melon balls—whatever you fancy. When it's all stirred in, taste for sweetness and add sugar to taste.

Pour the wine into a large pitcher. Stir in the sugar, and squeeze in the juices from the orange, lemon, and lime wedges. Pour in the brandy, toss in some of the fruit wedges, and chill for at least 4 hours. Pour in the club soda just before serving.

Wassail

Yield: 15 cups

This wonderful, festive punch really helps to warm and soothe you.

One 6-inch cinnamon stick, broken into 2 to 3 pieces

16 whole cloves, plus additional for studding the oranges

1 teaspoon whole allspice berries, lightly crushed

3 oranges, scrubbed

6 cups apple cider (not juice)

2 cups cranberry juice

¼ cup sugar, more or less, as needed

1 teaspoon Angostura Bitters

4 cups white rum

Tie the cinnamon stick, 16 of the cloves, and the allspice in cheesecloth. Stud the oranges with more cloves and cut them in half.

In a large saucepan, combine the cider, cranberry juice, sugar, and bitters, stirring well. Add the cheesecloth packet, and bring the mixture just to a light boil, then simmer, covered, for 10 minutes.

Add the rum, heat through, and remove the cheesecloth packet. Transfer to a heatproof punch bowl and serve hot with the clove-studded oranges floating in the punch.

Midori Sours

Yield: 1 Midori cocktail

These have a very deceptive mildness, so don't serve them around the pool.

¼ cup vodka

¼ cup Midori melon liqueur

2 tablespoons freshly squeezed lime juice

Shake all of the ingredients with ice in a cocktail shaker and strain into a martini glass.

Sade singing "Smooth Operator" is the perfect music while sipping a Midori Sour and totally relaxing. It's one of Lucky and Lennie's go-to drinks. At times you can throw in a track or two of Amy Winehouse—always a trip.

The Venus Lychee Martini

Yield: 2 Martinis

This delicious martini is based on my memory of a lychee martini served at Kittichai, a Thai restaurant in Manhattan's SoHo. If you can't find superfine sugar, buzz ¼ cup regular, granulated sugar in a mini processor until it's finely ground to help it dissolve more easily in the liquids.

¼ cup superfine sugar

¼ cup filtered or bottled still water

1 cup drained bottled or canned lychees (about 18), 2 reserved for garnish

2 tablespoons freshly squeezed lemon juice

1 cup good-quality vodka

¼ cup Cointreau

In a 1-quart saucepan, dissolve the sugar in the water over high heat, stirring constantly. Pour the result into a heatproof bowl set in a larger bowl of ice water. Stir the sugar syrup occasionally, until the mixture is cold, about 5 minutes.

In the jar of a blender, purée the lychees in the sugar syrup with the lemon juice. Strain the mixture back into the sugar-water bowl. Discard any solids that remain in the strainer.

Fill a cocktail shaker halfway with ice cubes, pour in the lychee mixture, vodka, and Cointreau. Shake for 20 to 30 seconds, and strain into chilled martini glasses. Add 2 whole lychees for decoration.

Venus, boy toy in tow, entered Mr Chow restaurant in Beverly Hills like a true superstar. Blond, beautiful, her look polished to a diamond gloss. The paparazzi leapt to attention, flashbulbs popping overtime.

The young stud accompanying her attempted to look nonchalant, but there was no mistaking the look of triumph burning brightly in his eyes. A month ago he was a busboy in an Italian restaurant. Now he was on the arm of a very famous woman indeed—Venus—a star of epic proportions.

Chris, the handsome maître d', leapt forward and led them to a prime table. Conversations stopped. Heads turned. Venus settled into her seat. Within seconds Riccardo delivered her favorite lychee martini to the table.

Venus didn't have to ask. She merely had to enjoy.

Appetizers

Amazing Caesar Salad

Max's Beet and Avocado Salad

Mandarin Orange and Red Onion Salad with Champagne

Chorizo-Chocolate Tapas

Mushroom and Gruyère Tart

Creamy Macaroni and Cheese

Smoked Duck Pizza with Hoisin Sauce

Pizza with Mushroom and Sausage

Gino's Favorite Pesto Pizza

Smoked Salmon Pizza

Amazing Caesar Salad

(Lucky and Lennie's Favorite Late-Night Indulgence)

Yield: 3 to 4 large servings

CROUTONS

One 14- to 16-ounce loaf French or Italian peasant bread, sourdough if you like

4 tablespoons (½ stick) unsalted butter, melted

¼ cup extra-virgin olive oil

1 teaspoon kosher salt

Several dashes of Tabasco sauce

Several grinds of black pepper

SALAD

3 garlic cloves

4 anchovy fillets, rinsed

Kosher salt, to taste

1 teaspoon freshly ground black pepper

1 tablespoon freshly squeezed lemon juice

1 teaspoon Worcestershire

1 tablespoon red wine vinegar, with at least 6 percent acidity

2 teaspoons smooth Maille Dijon mustard

2 very fresh large egg yolks

½ cup extra-virgin olive oil

1 large head romaine lettuce

1 cup freshly grated Parmigiano-Reggiano cheese

12 white anchovies or boquerónes

This version has a crisp garlic bite and a certain earnestness of anchovies. Try to time the making of the croutons so that they will still be just warm when they're tossed with the rest of the salad to take any remaining chill out of the romaine.

For the croutons: Preheat the oven to 450°F. Remove the crusts from the loaf and cut the bread into ¾-inch cubes. In a very large bowl, combine the butter, oil, salt, Tabasco, and black pepper. Add the bread cubes and toss with your clean hands until the cubes are well coated. Spread the cubes out on a large, aluminum foil–lined baking sheet. Bake for about 10 minutes, or until just browned. (Reserve but don't bother to rinse the bowl.)

For the salad: Assemble the salad in private or in public. Pass the garlic through a garlic press into the same large bowl. Add the anchovy fillets and the salt and, using two forks, mash with the garlic into a paste. Whisk in the pepper, lemon juice, Worcestershire sauce, vinegar, mustard, and egg yolks. Finally, whisk in the olive oil until well blended.

Cut the romaine leaves into 1½-inch pieces. Add the warm croutons, romaine, and cheese to the bowl, toss well, and taste—extra cheese might be nice. Serve at once on individual salad plates, with 3 to 4 whole white anchovies draped over the top of each salad.

Max's Beet and Avocado Salad

Whisk together the vinegar, shallots, and honey in a large bowl, then slowly whisk in the olive oil to emulsify the vinaigrette. Season to taste with salt and pepper.

Toss the arugula, walnuts, and cooked beets with the vinaigrette. Arrange on individual plates, top with avocado cubes and crumbled goat cheese, and serve.

3 tablespoons balsamic vinegar

1 small shallot, very thinly sliced

2 teaspoons honey

¼ cup extra-virgin olive oil

Kosher salt

Freshly ground black pepper

5 medium cooked beets, quartered and sliced into bite-size pieces

5 cups baby arugula

¾ cup walnuts, toasted then coarsely chopped

1 avocado, halved, pitted, cubed, and peeled

4 ounces goat cheese, coarsely crumbled

"I can make it," Max, Lucky's teenage daughter, insisted.
"You can make what?" Lucky asked, amused.
"Dinner!" Max insisted.
Lucky raised an eyebrow.
"What?" Max fumed. "Don't you think I'm capable?"
"Of course you are," Lucky said. "After all, aren't I the one that taught you the motto 'Girls can do anything'?"
Max grinned. "Sit back and just you wait."
And that's how Max's Beet and Avocado Salad became one of the most popular dishes in the Santangelo household.

Mandarin Orange and Red Onion Salad with Champagne

Yield: 6 to 8 servings

The festive colors in this salad, to say nothing of the champagne finish, make it ideal for a celebratory meal.

In a medium bowl, whisk together the vinegar, orange zest, brown sugar, salt, and pepper. Whisk in the oil gradually to emulsify the vinaigrette.

About 30 minutes before serving, in a small bowl, toss the red onion with 2 tablespoons of the dressing. Cover and set aside.

Cut the endive crosswise into ½-inch-wide pieces. Separate the pieces into strips, discarding any tough, solid, center pieces.

When ready to serve, in a large bowl, toss the leaf vegetables with the remaining dressing. Top each portion with orange segments and red onions, then sprinkle with the cranberries. Pour the champagne over the salad, toss again, and serve.

¼ cup balsamic vinegar

Finely grated zest of 1 orange

1 tablespoon brown sugar

½ teaspoon Kosher salt

¼ teaspoon freshly ground black pepper

¾ cup olive oil

1 small red onion, thinly sliced

1 large head (or 2 small heads) endive, wiped with a moist cloth (do not rinse)

1 large head red leaf lettuce, torn into bite-size pieces

1 medium head radicchio, torn into bite-size pieces

Two 12-ounce cans mandarin oranges, well drained

½ cup dried cranberries

½ cup good-quality champagne

Chorizo-Chocolate Tapas

Yield: 4 to 6 appetizers

The idea of chocolate and cured sausage seems bizarre, at best, but the last time I was in Barcelona, this tapa was offered with four o'clock cocktails, and it's simply sensational. Like many wonderful Spanish dishes, it's also extremely easy! Currently, the only Spanish chorizo allowed to be sold in America is Palacios, which comes in hot (red string) or sweet (white string).

One 10- to 12-inch Palacios chorizo, preferably "hot"

1 baguette

Bittersweet chocolate spread, or Nutella chocolate-hazelnut spread

Saffron (optional)

Slice the chorizo crosswise into ⅛-inch disks. Slice the baguette into ¼-inch thick slices. Spread the bread with bittersweet chocolate and place 1 to 2 chorizo slices on the chocolate. Finish with 1 thread of saffron if desired.

Ah . . . Barcelona. Whenever Lucky's trusty assistant, Danny, thinks of Spain, he is reminded of his honeymoon with Buff—the man of his dreams. Lucky paid for their honeymoon, and both Danny and Buff made the most of every moment—especially chomping down Chorizo-Chocolate Tapas, a taste thrill indeed.

Mushroom and Gruyère Tart

Yield: 6 appetizer servings

Many of my regular dinner guests simply expect this tart, sliced into manageable wedges, to make the rounds before dinner. One even told me that she wouldn't consider one of my dinners complete without it.

½ cup whole-milk ricotta cheese

¼ cup whole-milk cottage cheese

2 large egg yolks

2 teaspoons plus 2 tablespoons olive oil

¼ cup crème fraîche

1½ pounds shiitake mushroom caps, sliced

2 teaspoons fresh thyme leaves

Kosher salt

Freshly ground black pepper

2 tablespoons soft, unsalted butter

1 cup thinly sliced scallions, white and light green parts only

1 sheet frozen puff pastry (half of a 17.3-ounce package), thawed at room temperature for 20 to 30 minutes, and chilled

1 large egg yolk, lightly beaten with 1 tablespoon cool water, for glazing

4 ounces thinly sliced or grated Gruyère cheese

Preheat the oven to 400°F. In a food processor, purée the ricotta with the cottage cheese until smooth, about 1 minute. Add 2 egg yolks and 2 teaspoons of the oil and blend. Transfer the mixture to a bowl, fold in the crème fraîche and mix well. Set aside.

Heat the remaining 2 tablespoons olive oil in a large, heavy-bottomed skillet over medium-high heat. Add the mushrooms and sauté for about 7 minutes. Mix in the thyme. Season to taste with salt and pepper. Add the butter and sauté until the mushrooms are tender, about 4 minutes more. Stir in the scallions and turn off the heat.

On a lightly floured surface, roll out the puff pastry into a rectangle about 13 × 9-inches. Using a sharp knife, and starting ¼ inch from the edge, cut a score line around the entire perimeter of the dough, cutting just halfway through. Brush the border with the egg glaze. Transfer the dough to an ungreased baking sheet. Spread the ricotta mixture over the dough, keeping it inside the egg-glazed border. Top with half of the mushrooms, half of the Gruyère, then the remaining mushrooms and Gruyère. Bake the tart until the crust is golden and the Gruyère has melted into the mushrooms, about 25 minutes.

Remove from oven and let rest for about ten minutes. Best when served warm.

Creamy Macaroni and Cheese

Yield: 4 servings

If you're going to make good macaroni and cheese, don't settle for anything low-fat, just have a smaller portion. Less is more!

Position an oven rack in the upper third of the oven, and preheat the oven to 375°F. Using 1 tablespoon of the butter, grease a 9-inch round or square baking pan, or a large 2½-quart enameled cast-iron gratin dish, especially if you want a nice dark crust to form at the bottom of the macaroni and cheese.

Put the cottage cheese, milk, mustard, cayenne, nutmeg, salt, and pepper in a large bowl. Purée the mixture using an immersion blender. Reserve ¼ cup of the grated cheese for topping, and stir the remaining cheese into the cottage cheese–milk mixture. Stir in the uncooked elbow macaroni. Pour the mixture into the buttered dish, cover tightly with aluminum foil, and bake for 30 minutes.

Uncover the pan, stir gently, sprinkle with the reserved cheese, and dot with the remaining 1 tablespoon butter. Bake, uncovered, 25 to 30 minutes more until browned and bubbling. Let cool at least 10 minutes. Before serving, dapple the macaroni and cheese very lightly with white truffle oil.

2 tablespoons unsalted butter

1 cup cottage cheese (not low-fat)

2 cups whole milk (not skim or low-fat)

2 teaspoons dry mustard

Pinch of cayenne

Pinch of freshly grated nutmeg

½ teaspoon kosher salt

¼ teaspoon freshly ground black pepper

1 pound sharp or extra-sharp cheddar cheese, grated

½ pound elbow pasta, uncooked

White truffle oil, for serving (optional)

Smoked Duck Pizza with Hoisin Sauce

Yield: one pizza

Hoisin sauce is now widely available in supermarkets. It gives this pizza a delicious depth of flavor.

¼ cup hoisin sauce

3 tablespoons oyster sauce

One 12-inch, prebaked, thin pizza crust, such as Boboli

½ medium red onion, thinly sliced

¼ pound smoked duck breast, thinly sliced

4 ounces shredded Monterey Jack cheese (about 1 cup)

1 tablespoon coarsely chopped fresh cilantro

Crushed red pepper flakes

Position an oven rack to the lowest position in the oven, line the bottom of the oven with aluminum foil to catch any spills, and preheat the oven to 450°F.

In a small bowl, blend the hoisin and oyster sauces and brush the top of the pizza crust with the mixture. Top with the red onion slices. Arrange the smoked duck breast in a circle on top and sprinkle with the cheese.

Place the pizza directly on the oven rack and bake until golden and crisp, 5 to 7 minutes. Sprinkle liberally with cilantro and red pepper flakes, cut into slices with a pizza wheel, and serve.

Delicious. Especially when accompanied by a rich red wine and some smooth Latin sounds. Lucky is totally into Marc Anthony and Ricky Martin. Great music to go with a great pizza!

Pizza with Mushroom and Sausage

Yield: 2 pizzas

If you're in a rush, you can use thin, prebaked, store-bought crusts, but the finished pizza won't be as good as when made with fresh dough. You can get a ball of fresh dough from any decent pizzeria for around a dollar.

One 16-ounce ball fresh pizza dough

1½ tablespoons olive oil

3 Italian sausages, casings removed

1 small red onion, thinly sliced

8 ounces fresh wild mushrooms, such as shiitakes and chanterelles, thickly sliced

2¼ teaspoons finely chopped fresh rosemary leaves

Kosher salt

Freshly ground black pepper

⅔ cup finely grated Parmigiano-Reggiano cheese

½ teaspoon crushed red pepper flakes

1¾ cups coarsely grated whole-milk mozzarella cheese, about a ½ pound

Position one oven rack in the top third of the oven and one rack in the bottom third of the oven and preheat the oven to 450°F. Lightly flour two baking sheets. Place the dough on a work surface and let it stand until it reaches room temperature, about 20 minutes.

While the dough rests, heat 1 tablespoon of the oil in a large nonstick skillet over medium-high heat. Add the sausage meat and sauté, breaking it into ½-inch pieces with the back of a spoon, until browned about 5 minutes. Using a slotted spoon, transfer the sausage to a bowl. Discard some of the fat left behind in the skillet (if you wish). Add the onion and sauté until just tender, about 2 minutes. Transfer to a plate. Add the remaining ½ tablespoon olive oil to the skillet and toss in the mushrooms and ¾ teaspoon of the rosemary. Sprinkle with salt and black pepper and sauté until brown, about 5 minutes. Transfer to the plate with the onion.

Divide the dough into two pieces. Press and stretch each piece out on a lightly floured work surface or dough board into a 5-inch round. Sprinkle each round with ⅓ cup of the Parmigiano-Reggiano, ¾ teaspoon of the rosemary, and the red pepper flakes; then sprinkle each with kosher salt. Using a floured rolling pin, roll out each piece of dough into a 10-inch round, pressing in the seasonings. Transfer the dough rounds to the prepared baking sheets. Leaving ½-inch border, top each dough round with ¾ cup of the mozzarella, then divide the onion, sausage, and mushrooms equally between the rounds.

Bake the pizzas until the bottoms of the crusts are crisp and brown, reversing the baking sheets after 10 minutes, about 20 minutes total. Using a large spatula, transfer the pizzas to a work surface and sprinkle each with 2 tablespoons more of the mozzarella. Slice the pizzas with a large chef's knife—a pizza wheel cutter can drag the toppings in this recipe. Serve at once.

Gino's Favorite Pesto Pizza

Yield: one pizza

A verdant, rich treat, to be sure, and quite easy to pull together. Note that the prebaked pizza crust should be thin.

Preheat the oven to 450°F.

For the pesto: Wash and thoroughly dry the basil leaves. Put the basil, olive oil, pine nuts, garlic, and an ample pinch of salt in the bowl of a food processor, and process to a creamy consistency.

Transfer the pesto to a bowl and mix in the grated cheese by hand. When the cheese is evenly blended with the other ingredients, mix in the softened butter with a fork, distributing it uniformly into the sauce.

For the pizza: Place the pizza crust on a baking sheet. Spread the pesto evenly across the crust, crumble the goat cheese over all, arrange the anchovies decoratively, and sprinkle with the oregano. Bake watchfully until the cheese melts, 10 to 12 minutes, or according to the manufacturer's instructions.

Max's favorite. She especially loves sitting around the kitchen with her friends, Cookie and Harry, after a night of fun. Clubbing can be exhausting, so late-night pizza is just the dish to revive them. With Gaga and Pitbull on the iPod, they are ready to party again. And Max *loves* to party.

PESTO

2 cups tightly packed fresh basil leaves

½ cup extra-virgin olive oil

3 tablespoons pine nuts

2 garlic cloves, put through a garlic press, or very finely minced

Kosher salt

⅔ cup finely grated Parmigiano-Reggiano cheese

3 tablespoons unsalted butter, softened to room temperature

PIZZA

1 prebaked, 12-inch thin pizza crust, such as Boboli

½ cup pesto

3½- to 4-ounce (small) log of soft goat cheese, such as chèvre

12 anchovy fillets (or more), well rinsed

1 teaspoon dried oregano

Smoked Salmon Pizza

Yield: one pizza

A truly delicious concoction that comes together quickly. This makes an ideal lunch dish and an equally ideal late-night snack.

One 12-inch, thin, prebaked pizza crust, such as Boboli

½ cup mascarpone cheese

½ cup softened cream cheese

½ pound sliced smoked salmon

Chopped fresh dill, as desired

Freshly ground black or white pepper

Preheat the oven to 350°F.

Warm the pizza crust on the upper rack of the oven. Remove from the oven and let cool slightly.

Meanwhile, in a medium bowl, combine the mascarpone and cream cheese with an immersion blender until fluffy and spreadable. When the pizza crust has cooled a bit, spread the cheese mixture evenly over the pizza, leaving a ½-inch border all the way around.

Arrange the salmon slices over the cheese mixture, overlapping if necessary. Sprinkle with fresh dill to taste, and finish with a good grinding of black or white pepper.

This amazing pizza is everyone's favorite! The combination of the smoked salmon and tangy cream cheese is a crowd pleaser. Gino gew up eating pizza—not quite as fancy as the smoked salmon special. At times he prefers to eat old-school—listening to Frank Sinatra and Dean Martin while he munches away.

Pasta Appetizers

Lemon Linguine

Rigatoni with Bacon and Shiitake Mushrooms

Penne alla Vodka Martini with Tomato, Sausage, Bacon, and Cream

Pasta Puttanesca

Angel Hair Pasta with Sweet Sausage, Saffron, and Cream

Lasagne with Wild Mushrooms, Sausage, Four Cheeses, and Prosciutto

Veal Saffron Cream Pasta Sauce

Fettuccine with Crab and Cream

Fettuccine with Clams and Chorizo

Rigatoni with Lobster Champagne Cream

Lemon Linguine

Yield: 4 servings

This dish is as zippy as it is comforting if you're feeling fragile.

6 tablespoons (¾ stick) unsalted butter

½ cup dried bread crumbs

2 large egg yolks

½ cup heavy cream

½ cup finely grated Parmigiano-Reggiano cheese

Finely grated zest of 1 lemon and juice of ½ lemon, plus more juice as needed

Pinch of kosher salt

Freshly ground black pepper

1 pound linguine

2 tablespoons minced flat-leaf parsley

Melt 2 tablespoons of the butter in a small skillet over medium heat. Add the bread crumbs and cook, stirring, until toasted. Set aside.

Bring a large pot of water to a boil and season with salt. Add the pasta and cook according to the package directions until al dente.

While the pasta cooks, in a bowl, using a fork, blend the yolks, cream, cheese, lemon zest and juice, salt, and pepper. Taste the sauce and if you want it more lemony, stir in more juice as needed.

When the pasta is just al dente, remove and reserve a cup of the pasta water, drain the pasta, and return it to the pot. Throw in the remaining 4 tablespoons butter and stir and swirl until the pasta is well coated.

Stir in the egg mixture and turn the pasta in it, adding a few table-spoons of the reserved pasta water if it looks a bit dry.

Place in serving bowls and sprinkle with the parsley and the toasted bread crumbs.

This linguine is great for that lingering hangover that takes you by surprise. It's a Santangelo family favorite.

Rigatoni with Bacon and Shiitake Mushrooms

Yield: 4 servings

Pasta is the best dinner party dish. There's always plenty to go around, and everyone loves it. If you've got a vegetarian on board, simply leave out the bacon or pancetta—which is why I could never be a vegetarian! The crème fraîche gives the dish a certain tanginess. It wouldn't be the same without it. Don't use sour cream instead—it tends to separate when cooked.

Bring a large pot of water to a boil and season with about 1 tablespoon of sea salt per quart of water. Add the rigatoni to the pot and cook until al dente, 8 to 10 minutes.

While the pasta cooks, mash the sage, rosemary, and garlic together to form a thick paste. Set aside.

Warm a large sauté pan over medium heat, add the chopped bacon, and cook, stirring occasionally, until some fat has rendered and it begins to brown and crisp, about 6 minutes. Add the sliced shiitake mushrooms and cook for 4 minutes, stirring occasionally. Add the sage-rosemary-garlic mixture, stir well, and cook for 2 minutes. Add the splash of vermouth and deglaze the pan with a wooden spoon. Add the tomatoes, stir, and cook 3 minutes. Add the crème fraîche and butter and stir to incorporate.

By now the rigatoni should be al dente. Drain and add it to the sauté pan. Add the cheese and parsley, and season with pepper. Serve promptly.

Sea salt

1 pound dried rigatoni or penne rigate

2 fresh sage leaves, finely chopped

3 sprigs fresh rosemary, needles removed from stems and finely chopped

1 garlic clove, smashed and peeled

½ pound sliced bacon or pancetta, cut into ¼-inch wedges

½ pound sliced shiitake mushroom caps

Splash of dry white vermouth or white wine

4 plum tomatoes, fresh or canned, seeded and chopped

1 cup crème fraîche

2 tablespoons unsalted butter

½ cup freshly grated Parmigiano-Reggiano cheese

2 tablespoons minced flat-leaf parsley

Freshly ground black pepper

Penne alla Vodka Martini with Tomato, Sausage, Bacon, and Cream

Yield: 4 large servings, but great for 2, because the leftovers are particularly succulent

I always thought penne alla vodka needed the buttery, slightly herbal lilt of vermouth. This incredibly rich, voluptuous pasta loves to be practically covered with vegetable-peeler curls of Parmigiano-Reggiano. The choice of bacon or pancetta at the outset is completely up to you: Bacon lends a light smoky flavor; pancetta is more, well, Italian—lots of body with nice rich insinuations.

Try to find a brand of crushed plum tomatoes that is not packed in tomato purée, which can make the sauce too thick. Muir Glen crushed tomatoes are very good, but if you can find real imported San Marzano tomatoes, lunge. And you can always "crush your own" right in the can with a trusty fork.

It takes a certain vigilance to stir and reduce the sauce for the last 10 minutes over spittingly high heat, but it's worth it, believe me. But if you haven't got a splatter screen, then God bless you.

The pasta-to-sauce ratio would make true Italians wince. Too bad.

¼ pound slab bacon, cut into ¼-inch pieces or ¼ pound pancetta, cut into ¼-inch pieces

1 large onion, chopped

1 teaspoon crushed red pepper flakes, plus more if desired

One 28-ounce can crushed San Marzano plum tomatoes

About 2 pounds sweet Italian sausage, the best you can get; fennel-free, if possible

In a deep, heavy-bottomed sauté pan, cook the bacon or pancetta over moderate heat until most of the fat has rendered. Pour off all but 2 tablespoons of the fat (or as you wish), add the onion and red pepper flakes, and cook just until the onion is soft and translucent. Add the tomatoes, lower the heat, and simmer for 30 minutes, stirring every 5 to 10 minutes.

Meanwhile, bring 4 quarts of water to the boil in a large pot. Prick the sausages with a pin every inch or so and toss them into the water. Bring them to a simmer and let them bubble away for 10 minutes. Drain the sausages and cool them in a colander.

Meanwhile, bring a large pot of salted water to a boil for the penne, which will probably need no more than 10 to 12 minutes to cook, so don't add it to the boiling water until the final phase.

Add the vodka, vermouth, and tomato paste to the tomato mixture. Simmer for 15 minutes. Cut the cooled sausages into bite-size pieces and toss them into the sauce. Just when you're ready to add the penne to the boiling water, increase the heat under the sauce to high, add the cream, and, using a splatter screen as needed, and stirring often, boil the sauce vigorously for 10 minutes, about the amount of time the pasta needs to cook. The sauce will, of course, thicken considerably.

You can blend the cooked penne with the sauce, stirring in the grated cheese, oregano, and red pepper flakes, if using. Serve garnished with the shaved curls of Parmigiano-Reggiano.

OR

Preheat the broiler. Drain the pasta and, without rinsing, transfer it to a 2½-quart (or larger) gratin dish. Add the sauce and stir in grated cheese to taste, the oregano, and the red pepper flakes, if using. Place the dish under the broiler and cook just until the penne poking out of the top of the gratin begin to singe and crisp and the sauce sizzles, 2 to 4 minutes. Serve topped with the shaved curls of Parmigiano-Reggiano.

¾ cup vodka

½ cup French dry vermouth

3 tablespoons tomato paste

1 cup heavy cream

1 pound good-quality dried penne rigate

Plenty of Parmigiano-Reggiano cheese, some freshly grated and some shaved with a vegetable peeler, for garnish

Oregano, chopped fresh or dried

One of the reasons Lucky and Lennie have such a great marriage is separation. Yes, being apart from each other! While both are committed to their careers, they come together with a vengeance. They share a great friendship, an incredible sex life, and an unsurpassed craving for adventure. Temptation is always around both of them, but to succumb to temptation is to open a door that eventually leads to an exit. Lucky and Lennie both realize what they have, and neither of them would ever dream of tempting fate.

Togetherness and loyalty rule in the Santangelo household.

Pasta Puttanesca

Yield: 4 servings

The origins of this Roman sauce are murky, if you're expected to believe all the explanations. I'm sure I don't have to tell you what a puttana is, but the main story holds that prostitutes needed a very quick sauce so they could get to work. Another story holds that the sauce, bubbling away, creates a scent that those looking for a lady of the night could not resist.

This sauce works with spaghetti, linguine, or perciatelli. The finished dish comes together very quickly—in the time it takes for the pasta to cook, about 11 minutes. Be sure to reserve the tomato juices when you drain the tomatoes from the can. They're for the naked pasta.

2 tablespoons kosher salt

1 pound spaghetti, linguine, or perciatelli

4 garlic cloves, pressed into a glass measure, covered with 1 tablespoon water

2 tablespoons olive oil

1 teaspoon crushed red pepper flakes, or droplets of Tabasco sauce

8 to 10 anchovy fillets, rinsed and finely minced (or use a mortar and pestle)

One 28-ounce can organic diced, roasted tomatoes, drained, juices reserved

3 tablespoons capers, rinsed and drained

¾ cup black olives (Gaeta, Alfonso, and/or Kalamata), pitted and coarsely chopped

¼ cup minced flat-leaf parsley leaves

Bring 6 quarts of water to a boil. Prepare and assemble the ingredients as described to the left and line them all up on your countertop.

When the water reaches a rolling boil, add 2 tablespoons of salt and the pasta. Stir after a few minutes to keep the pasta from sticking together.

Immediately heat the oil, garlic mixture, red pepper flakes, and anchovies in a large skillet over medium heat. Cook, stirring frequently, until the garlic is fragrant but not brown, 2 to 3 minutes. Stir in the tomatoes and simmer until slightly thickened, about 8 minutes.

Cook the pasta until al dente. Drain, then return the pasta to the pot. Add ½ cup (or so) of the reserved tomato juices to the pasta and toss quickly to combine.

Stir the capers, olives, and parsley into the sauce. Pour the sauce over the pasta and toss to combine, adding more of the reserved tomato juice to moisten, if necessary.

Serve immediately.

Angel Hair Pasta with Sweet Sausage, Saffron, and Cream

Yield: 4 servings

Allow 80 to 90 minutes to make this, to allow all the flavors to come together.

In a medium, heavy-bottomed skillet, melt the butter over medium-high heat. Add the onions and cook until they are soft and have lost their moisture. Reduce the heat to medium-low, and continue to cook so that the onions brown slowly, stirring frequently, until dark brown but not burned, about 45 minutes total cooking time. It may be necessary to adjust the heat to prevent them from burning. When the onions are a deep mahogany, scrape them into a huge heatproof bowl.

Heat the olive oil in the same skillet. Crumble the sausage into the oil and cook, stirring occasionally, over medium-high heat until lightly browned. Don't let the meat dry out. Add the cream and saffron, and stir for 2 minutes. Return the onions to the sausage mixture.

Meanwhile, bring a large pot of salted water to a boil. Add the peas, if using, to the onion and sausage mixture. Add the pasta to the boiling water and cook until al dente, following the package directions. Reserve some of the pasta water and drain the pasta. Add the pasta to the sausage mixture along with a splash of the reserved water, if necessary, but the sauce should not be wet or runny. The angel hair should be well coated and shiny from the sauce. Transfer to serving dishes, and season with plenty of cracked pepper and grated cheese. Serve immediately.

8 tablespoons (1 stick) unsalted butter

4 medium or 2 large onions, cut into ½-inch pieces

1 tablespoon olive oil

1 pound sweet Italian sausage, casings removed

¼ cup heavy cream

8 strands saffron

Kosher salt

Freshly ground black pepper

One 10-ounce package frozen petite peas, not defrosted (optional)

1 pound angel hair pasta

Plenty of freshly cracked black pepper

Freshly grated Parmigiano-Reggiano cheese

Lasagne with Wild Mushrooms, Sausage, Four Cheeses, and Prosciutto

Yield: about 10 servings

SAUCE

3 tablespoons olive oil

3 medium garlic cloves, minced

3 medium onions, well chopped

2 tablespoons extra-virgin olive oil

2½ pounds sweet Italian sausage, preferably without fennel, casings removed

1½ pounds ground beef chuck

1 cup whole milk

32 ounces your favorite bottled tomato sauce (Rao's or Muir Glen with Romano Cheese)

One 28-ounce can whole tomatoes and their juices, squished by hand (preferably Muir Glen)

One 14-ounce can diced tomatoes and their liquid (preferably Muir Glen)

2 tablespoons chopped fresh basil, if available (dried basil has little flavor)

1 teaspoon dried oregano

2 teaspoons chopped fresh thyme, or 1 teaspoon dried thyme

Don't be intimidated by all the ingredients. This recipe can feed ten hungry people. Because this crowd-thrilling lasagne has to bake for only 45 minutes and rest for just 15, you can prepare it up to an hour before your guests arrive, and put it in the oven during the first round of cocktails. But keep in mind that the sauce needs to be started 3 to 4 hours in advance.

To make things easier, use a disposable "medium roaster" aluminum pan, approximately 16 × 11 × 3 inches. Support the bottom with a baking sheet, of course.

This recipe uses "no-boil" lasagne noodles, which rehydrate rather thirstily, so don't be stingy with the wines.

For the sauce: Set a large, heavy-bottomed saucepan over medium heat. Add the olive oil, garlic, and onions and sweat until the onions are very soft, 10 to 15 minutes. Remove all but about 4 tablespoons of this mixture and reserve it for the filling.

To the saucepan with the 4 tablespoons of onion mixture, add the sausage and ground chuck and brown, breaking the meat up and stirring with a wooden spoon. Season with salt. When the last pinkness in the meat begins to disappear, drain the fat, as desired. Add the milk and boil gently until the milk has evaporated and virtually vanished, about 15 minutes.

Add the remaining sauce ingredients, stirring, and taste carefully. Simmer the sauce, partially covered, for at least 3 hours. The mixture should seem a bit soupy as it goes along; add wine if it's not. The noodles will absorb a lot of liquid.

For the filling: First, rinse the dried porcinis and soak in hot water for at least 20 minutes. Place the reserved onion mixture in a large, deep sauté pan over medium heat and refresh with 2 to 3 tablespoons fresh olive oil. Add sliced fresh mushrooms to the pan, and cook for 2 minutes, stirring, just until they release their liquid.

Remove the rehydrated porcinis from warm water and set aside. Pour the water through a very fine sieve into a cup to remove the grit, and pour the liquid into the pan. Chop the porcinis well and add them to the pan of fresh mushrooms along with the rosemary. Cook until the liquid is absorbed, a few minutes. Add the Marsala and cook for a few minutes to reduce.

Transfer the mixture to a large bowl, add the ricotta, Parmigiano-Reggiano, nutmeg, eggs, and black pepper and mix well. Set aside.

Taste the sauce carefully. Adjust the seasoning, adding more tomato paste, salt, and/or even a jot of sugar, as needed.

Preheat the oven to 375°F. Butter an aluminum medium roaster pan and place on a baking sheet. Cover the bottom with two ladlefuls of sauce. Lay in a layer of lasagne noodles to fit, spread on about a third of the filling, sprinkle on the Jack cheese, dot with crème fraîche, then sauce again. Repeat the layering until all the ingredients are used, finishing with the last of the sauce. Layer the top with the prosciutto and ¼-inch wedges of fresh mozzarella. Sprinkle with oregano, if you wish. The lasagne can be assembled to this point and left to stand at room temperature for an hour before baking.

Bake at 375°F for 45 minutes, or until nice and bubbly. Let the lasagne rest for 15 minutes before cutting into wedges and serving.

½ cup dry French white vermouth

1 to 3 tablespoons tomato paste

FILLINGS
¾ cup dried porcini mushrooms

1 pound assorted sliced fresh wild mushrooms, especially shiitakes, chanterelles, and/or creminis

2 good pinches of crumbled dried rosemary

½ cup Marsala wine

2 pounds fresh ricotta cheese

¾ cup freshly grated Parmigiano-Reggiano cheese

10 to 15 fresh gratings of nutmeg

3 large eggs, lightly beaten

Freshly ground black pepper

Unsalted butter, for greasing the lasagne pan

1 pound grated Monterey Jack cheese

1 cup crème fraîche

½ pound sliced prosciutto (di Parma, if possible), torn into bite-size pieces

1 pound fresh mozzarella, for topping

About ¾ pound No-Boil Lasagne Noodles (Delverde brand preferred)

Veal Saffron Cream Pasta Sauce

Yield: 3 to 4 servings

This is loosely based on a recipe by Marcella Hazan, but I've adapted it heavily, and increased the quantities of some of the ingredients enough to make Hazan bite her lip. The sauce works best with fresh pasta, but it's so good you can use it on any pasta at all.

2 tablespoons unsalted butter

1 tablespoon canola oil

¼ cup chopped onion

1½ pounds ground veal

Kosher salt

Freshly ground black pepper

¼ teaspoon ground saffron, or ⅓ teaspoon saffron strands, chopped

1 cup heavy cream

Freshly grated Parmigiano-Reggiano cheese

1 pound of fresh tricolor "honey-comb" pasta, or fresh pappardelle

Put the butter, oil, and onion in a skillet or sauté pan over medium-high heat and cook until the onion is a pale gold color. Add the ground veal and cook, crumbling it with a fork or potato masher and turning it from time to time, until it has browned all over. Season with salt and a liberal grinding of pepper, turning the meat 2 to 3 times.

Add the saffron and cream and reduce the heat to medium. Cook the cream down, stirring frequently, until it is no longer runny.

Meanwhile, drop the pasta into a large pot of abundantly salted water. The moment it is tender but still firm to the bite, drain it and toss it immediately with the sauce. Serve at once, with grated Parmigiano-Reggiano on the side.

Oh yeah! And after you're done eating, sit down and watch *The Godfather* trilogy on DVD. You will not regret it!

Fettuccine with Crab and Cream

Yield: 4 servings

This is about as rich as it gets. It's also intensely delicious with lobster meat instead of crab. If, for some reason, you want to lighten it—well, make another recipe!

Combine 1⅓ cups of the cream and the butter in a sauté pan large enough to hold the cooked pasta. Heat over low until the butter has melted and the cream has come to a bare simmer. Turn off the heat and set aside.

Bring 4 quarts of water to a boil in a large pot. Add 1 tablespoon of salt and the pasta to the boiling water. Cook until just al dente, according to the package directions. Drain the pasta and add it to the sauté pan. Add the remaining ⅓ cup cream, the crabmeat, ½ teaspoon salt, and cayenne. Cook over very low heat, tossing to combine the ingredients, until the sauce is slightly thickened, 1 to 2 minutes. Serve at once.

1⅔ cups heavy cream

5 tablespoons (½ stick plus 1 tablespoon) unsalted butter

1 tablespoon plus ½ teaspoon kosher salt

1 pound fresh fettuccine, or fresh lasagna sheets rolled and cut crosswise into fettuccine ribbons

1 pound fresh lump crabmeat, or slightly less, drained and picked over to remove possible shell bits

Pinch of cayenne pepper

"Y'know," Lennie said, reaching for Lucky's hand as they lolled on the couch watching reruns of *Breaking Bad*, "Food can be very sexy!"
Lucky smiled. "As long as you don't stuff yourself—which you just did!"
"I know. But who can resist your fettuccine."
"Ah." Lucky purred. "So *that's* why you love me."
Lennie grinned—"You got it, babe."

Fettuccine with Clams and Chorizo

Yield: 2 main-course servings

Clams and chorizo sausage belong together like salt and pepper. This comes together fairly quickly. You can used frozen minced clams (not canned!), but the dish won't be the same.

2 dozen littleneck clams, well scrubbed, rinsed, and refrigerated for 6 to 8 hours in a bowl of cold salt water with 2 tablespoons cornmeal sprinkled over the surface

5 to 6 tablespoons kosher salt

2 tablespoons unsalted butter

1 red onion, finely chopped

1 large yellow bell pepper, stemmed, seeded, and diced

2 plum tomatoes, cored, seeded, and diced

6 to 8 ounces Spanish chorizo, such as Palacios, cut into a ¼-inch dice

8 ounces fettuccine

½ cup dry white vermouth

2 tablespoons olive oil

2 tablespoons chopped cilantro or Italian parsley, whichever you prefer

1 scallion, white and light green parts only, minced

Crushed red pepper flakes (optional)

Bring a large pot of about 6 quarts of water to a boil for the pasta. After it comes to a boil, salt the water well—5 to 6 tablespoons of kosher salt—and keep it hot.

Meanwhile, heat the butter over medium heat in a large skillet with a lid. Add the chopped onion and minced bell pepper and sauté, uncovered, for about 5 minutes, stirring often.

Add the chorizo and cook, uncovered, stirring often, for 3 minutes, or until just browned. Add the diced tomatoes and cook, stirring, for 3 minutes more.

Add the fettuccine to the boiling, salted water, stirring often to avoid clumping. (You have about 9 minutes.)

Increase the heat under the sausage mixture to high. Stir in the vermouth and add the clams to the bubbling sausage mixture. Bring to a simmer, shaking pan to make a single layer of clams, then cover and steam until the clams open, 7 to 8 minutes. (Discard any clams that do not open.)

Drain the pasta and divide it between two large bowls. Drizzle the sauce with olive oil, then ladle it generously over the pasta, with a dozen clams for each portion. Sprinkle on the cilantro or parsley and the scallions. Serve at once, with the red pepper flakes on the side, if desired.

Rigatoni with Lobster Champagne Cream

Yield: 4 servings

One of the more user-friendly lobster recipes—and one of the most romantic! I just love the way some of the rigatoni gets brown and crispy. It gives the final stirred dish such a nice texture.

1 pound ridged rigatoni

⅛ teaspoon freshly ground white pepper

2 tablespoons unsalted butter

1 cup heavy cream

½ cup good-quality champagne

2 tablespoons chopped fresh chervil, or 1 tablespoon finely minced fresh tarragon

1 teaspoon kosher salt

Four 6-ounce lobster tails, cooked, shelled, meat sliced into ½-inch coins

In a large pot of salted boiling water, cook the rigatoni until a little less than al dente, 10 to 11 minutes.

Meanwhile, make the sauce. In a medium saucepan over medium-high heat, combine the white pepper, butter, heavy cream, and champagne, stirring constantly, until the butter has completely melted and the sauce has thickened slightly, about 7 minutes. Reduce the heat to low.

Preheat the oven to 325°F. When the rigatoni is a little less than al dente, drain it thoroughly and transfer it to a 2½-quart gratin dish. Pour the cream sauce over the rigatoni and transfer the gratin dish to the oven. Bake for 10 to 12 minutes until the rigatoni on top starts to brown and crisp.

Remove the gratin dish from the oven and stir the chervil, salt, and lobster meat into the rigatoni mixture and toss until well combined. Serve at once.

Is there any sexier food than lobster smothered in a rich creamy sauce? I think not. And it is one of Lucky's favorite dishes. She makes it just for Lennie when he's home from a grueling location shoot and it's just the two of them, alone together.

The Importance of Creating a Mood

Let's talk table settings. Lucky is very casual, but I like to make things a little more formal, although still fun. If you are throwing a dinner party, make sure you plan ahead—there's nothing worse than having to put things together at the last minute. For example, if you want to set a beautiful table, the way to do it is the day before. I love a black and gold theme—gold placemats, black napkins, and a few Cartier panthers scattered around. Candles are a must, and look great in everything from silver candlestick holders to cut glass. And beautiful wineglasses make a table shine.

Lighting and music always create a mood. Low flattering lighting, and great music from the old classics to the very latest sounds. I highly recommend a combination of Adele, Usher, Sade, and Enrique. An unbeatable mix. Lucky and I share the same taste in music, so I know she would approve.

Invite an interesting mix of guests, and before you know it the wine is flowing, the food is amazing, and you've got a party going on!

Entrées

Zucchini Boats

Eggplant Parmesan

Deviled Chicken Drumsticks

Lucky's Special Southern Fried Chicken

Chicken Breasts with Fontina
and Prosciutto

Chicken Paella with Spanish Chorizo

Chicken Cacciatore

Bourbon Chicken Milanese

Grilled Lime Chicken with Fontina
Cheese and Dried Chile Sauce

Chicken Breasts with Roasted Lemon,
Green Olive, and Capers

Coq au Vin

Roasted Sage Sausages and Grapes

Duck Burgers with Onion Marmalade

Lucky's Get-You-Going Turkey

Pork Chops Milanese

Pork Chops Saltimbocca with
Sautéed Spinach

Pork Tenderloin with
Honey-Mustard Sauce

Pulled Pork Tacos

Sweet and Spicy Spareribs

Lucky's Luscious Meatballs

The Best Hamburger in Town!

Peppered Beef Stroganoff

Lucky's Kick-Ass Chili

Rococo Meat Loaf

Beef Tenderloin Steaks with
Brandy and Mustard Sauce

Steak Tartare

Roast Beef Dusted with Coriander

Bourbon-Marinated Flank Steak

Lamb Steaks with Mushrooms

Lamb You Can Eat with a Spoon

Roasted Veal Scallops with Vegetables

Shrimp in Lemony Coconut Milk

Santangelo Salmon

Skate with Lobster Rice

Sole with Parmesan Crust

Zucchini Boats

Yield: 6 servings

These are great time, money, and heat savers when zucchini is at its ubiquitous height-of-summer peak. Served at room temperature, zucchini have an appealing lightness, but they're also very filling, so one per person should be about right. This recipe makes six boats.

Place the whole, unpeeled zucchini in a large pot of rapidly boiling water. Cover and let boil for 15 minutes. Drain the squash and set aside to cool.

Melt the butter over medium heat, stir in the chopped onion, and sweat for 5 minutes. Add the rice, coriander, and cumin and stir until every grain is coated with the hot butter. Pour in the stock or water and the chorizo and bring just to a boil. Cover tightly, lower the heat to keep the rice at a simmer, and cook for 13 minutes.

When the rice is done, and while it's still hot, stir in the tomato sauce and the Parmigiano-Reggiano. Set the mixture aside to cool.

Cut each squash in half lengthwise and, using a small spoon, scoop out the seeds and discard, and then the flesh, reserving about half of the flesh, and leaving a shell in each zucchini about ½ inch thick. Sprinkle the shells with a little kosher salt and invert them in a sieve to drain for 10 minutes. Chop the reserved zucchini flesh and add it to the cooled rice mixture. Taste the rice carefully, and season with salt, pepper, and probably additional grated cheese if needed.

Place the zucchini shells on a small baking sheet and pat them dry with paper towels. Fill them with the rice mixture, sprinkle with the grated Jack cheese, and press the quartered cherry tomatoes into the rice mixture at attractive intervals. Run the zucchini boats under the broiler, just to melt the cheese, 1 to 2 minutes, then sprinkle with chopped parsley. Serve at room temperature.

3 fairly large uncurved zucchini

3 tablespoons unsalted butter

1 medium onion, finely chopped

1 cup long-grain white rice

2 teaspoons ground coriander

1 teaspoon ground cumin

2 cups chicken stock

2 to 3 cooked chorizo sausages (preferably Palacios), chopped into ¼-inch pieces

1 cup homemade or favorite bottled chunky tomato sauce

¾ to 1 cup freshly grated Parmigiano-Reggiano cheese

1 cup grated Monterey Jack cheese

2 tablespoons chopped flat-leaf parsley or cilantro, whichever you prefer

3 to 4 quartered cherry tomatoes

Eggplant Parmesan

Yield: 3 ample servings

Even people who claim to hate eggplant just devour this dish. Part of what makes it work so well is that white eggplant is much less bitter—and less likely to become slimy—than purple.

3 pounds white eggplant (about 3 medium-size eggplants)

Canola oil, for frying

All-purpose flour, for dredging

1 tablespoon olive oil

One 14-ounce can organic diced tomatoes, such as Muir Glen, with their juices

2 to 3 tablespoons kosher salt

1 pound fresh mozzarella (smoked, if you wish)

8 to 10 fresh basil leaves

Unsalted butter, for smearing and dotting the dish

½ cup freshly grated Parmigiano-Reggiano cheese

Peel the eggplants and slice crosswise into ⅜-inch pieces. Stand one layer of slices upright against the inside of a pasta colander and sprinkle both sides with kosher salt. Stand another layer of slices against the first and sprinkle with salt. Repeat until you have salted all the eggplant. Let the eggplant degorge for 30 minutes. Lightly rinse off the salt and pat each slice thoroughly dry with paper towels.

Select a large, fairly deep frying pan, set over high heat, and pour in 1 inch of the canola oil. Put the flour on a plate and dredge the eggplant slices in the flour, coating on both sides. Do only a few slices at a time, when you're ready to fry them. If the oil sizzles when you dip a corner of a slice in, it's ready. Slip as many of the slices into the pan as will fit loosely without overlapping. Cook to a golden brown on one side, then turn. Do not turn more than once. When they are all golden brown, transfer the eggplant to a wire rack set on a baking sheet. Repeat until all of the eggplant is cooked.

Meanwhile, put the olive oil and tomatoes into a saucepan over medium-high heat, add salt, stir, and cook the tomatoes down until reduced by half.

Position a rack in the upper third of the oven, and preheat the oven to 400°F. Cut the mozzarella into thin slices, and tear the basil leaves into 2 or 3 pieces.

Butter the bottom and sides of a 2½-quart gratin dish. Place enough fried eggplant slices to line the bottom of the dish in a single layer, spread some of the cooked tomatoes over them, cover with a layer of mozzarella, sprinkle liberally with grated Parmigiano-Reggiano, strew a few pieces of basil over it, and top with another layer of fried eggplant, making little stacks. Repeat the procedure, ending with a layer of eggplant on top, and any mozzarella that's left. Sprinkle with grated Parmesan, place the dish on the top oven rack, and roast until bubbly, about 40 minutes.

Deviled Chicken Drumsticks

Yield: 4 to 6 servings

These are just terrific served hot or at room temperature.

Position a rack in the upper third of the oven and preheat the oven to 450°F. Butter a rimmed baking sheet.

Pat the chicken dry with paper towels, then toss with the mustard in a bowl, until evenly coated.

Stir together the panko, cheese, cayenne, salt, and black pepper. Drizzle with the butter and toss.

Dredge each drumstick in the crumb mixture to coat, then arrange, without crowding, on the prepared baking sheet. Roast until the chicken is browned and cooked through, about 30 minutes.

12 chicken drumsticks (about 3 pounds total)

½ cup smooth Dijon mustard, such as Maille

¾ cup panko (Japanese-style bread crumbs)

¾ cup grated Parmigiano-Reggiano cheese

1 teaspoon cayenne pepper

½ teaspoon kosher salt

½ teaspoon freshly ground black pepper

3 tablespoons unsalted butter, melted

When Lucky's in the mood she'll throw together a last minute get-together with family and friends. Deviled Chicken Drumsticks are quick and easy—not to mention delicious! Play Jay-Z and Drake on your iPod, and you've got yourself a party, Santangelo style.

Lucky's Special Southern Fried Chicken

4 to 6 pounds chicken legs, thighs, and breasts

2 cups buttermilk

3 heaping tablespoons whole-grain Dijon mustard

2 teaspoons toasted mustard seeds

1 teaspoon smoked sweet paprika

1 teaspoon freshly ground black pepper

Droplets of jalapeño or regular Tabasco sauce

1½ cups self-rising flour

½ cup cornstarch

3 tablespoons baking powder

Kosher salt, a pinch or two

Freshly ground black pepper

2 tablespoons Bell's Seasoning

1 teaspoon dried, rubbed thyme, sage, and rosemary

2 large eggs, lightly whisked in a medium bowl

Cayenne pepper (optional)

About 4 cups (32 ounces) peanut oil (for crunchy chicken) or lard, if you want a very crunchy, brown crust

1 large yellow onion, sliced into ½-inch rings

Yield: 5 to 6 servings

I have friends who, when I invite them for dinner, beg me to make this fried chicken.

Wash the chicken and pat dry. Place in a large plastic bag fitted into a large bowl. In a 1-quart glass measure, mix the buttermilk, mustard, mustard seeds, paprika, black pepper, and jalapeño or Tabasco. Pour the marinade over the chicken, tie or seal the bag securely, and refrigerate for 24 hours, turning the bag when you can, at least 3 times.

Put flour, cornstarch, baking powder, salt, black pepper, Bell's seasoning, herbs, and cayenne in 2 large, doubled paper bags fitted inside a plastic supermarket bag; close the bag, and shake to combine the ingredients. Drop in the onion rings and shake to coat lightly. Transfer the onion rings to a large plate. Drop in half the chicken into each doubled bag, close the bags, and shake to coat the chicken completely. Place the coated chicken on a large wire rack set on a baking sheet. Repeat with the rest of the chicken. Let the chicken rest uncovered in the refrizerator for about 30 minutes after coating with the flour mixture.

Meanwhile, heat about ½-inch of your oil of choice over medium-high heat in two heavy-bottomed skillets with lids (preferably cast iron). Heat the oil to 350°F. Toss in the onion rings and fry for several minutes until golden brown, then remove the onions with tongs and transfer to paper towels. Carefully add the chicken to the oil, cover, and cook over medium to medium-high heat. Check after 6 minutes and adjust the heat if the chicken is browning too quickly. After about 10 minutes total, carefully turn all the chicken and cook, uncovered, for 10 to 12 minutes more. Using tongs, transfer the chicken to a clean wire rack. Serve "whenever."

Chicken Breasts with Fontina and Prosciutto

Yield: 3 to 4 servings

A fairly quick weeknight dish that has lightness, loads of flavor, and a dash of elegance.

Preheat the oven to 400°F. Place each breast between sheets of plastic wrap and pound lightly with a flat mallet to even out the thickness. Season the chicken with salt, pepper, and a judicious sprinkling of the garlic powder.

Put the seasoned flour in a medium bowl. Beat the eggs with a little more salt and pepper in a second bowl. Put the panko in a third bowl.

Dip each chicken breast first in flour, then in the egg mixture, and finally in the panko, pressing firmly to make the crumbs adhere. Let the chicken rest in the refrigerator for 30 minutes to 1 hour before cooking.

Pour the canola oil into a large, cast-iron skillet over medium heat and add the butter. When the butter sizzles, add the chicken. Cook for about 3 minutes, or until the crumbs are nicely browned, then turn the chicken and cook 3 minutes on the opposite side until golden brown. Cover each piece with a slice of prosciutto, and top with the cheese.

Transfer the skillet to the oven and bake the chicken for 8 to 10 minutes, until the cheese is melted and bubbly.

4 boneless, skinless chicken breast halves (about 1¼ pounds total)

Kosher salt

Freshly ground black pepper

Ground dry-roasted garlic, or garlic powder

½ cup all-purpose flour, seasoned with salt and pepper

2 large eggs

1 cup panko (Japanese-style bread crumbs)

1 tablespoon canola oil

3 tablespoons unsalted butter

½ pound sliced prosciutto

½ pound grated fontina cheese

Chicken Paella with Spanish Chorizo

Yield: 4 ample servings

Here again, don't be frightened away by the long list of ingredients. Most are quite readily available, and the dish comes together fairly rapidly.

This preparation is much tastier if you use bone-in, skin-on chicken thighs and legs cut into 1½- to 2-inch pieces. If you can't get kosher chicken, brine the chicken pieces for 3 hours in 2 quarts of water with ½ cup of kosher salt and ½ cup of sugar, before you marinate. You don't have to brine the chicken, but it will be juicier and will caramelize more evenly if you do.

MARINADE

¼ cup dry fino sherry, or dry white wine

⅓ cup olive oil

2 teaspoons ground cumin

1 teaspoon ground coriander

Plenty of freshly ground black pepper

1 tablespoon fresh thyme leaves, or 1 teaspoon dried

½ teaspoon Chinese five-spice powder

½ teaspoon freshly grated nutmeg

2 bay leaves

½ teaspoon crushed red pepper flakes

3 tablespoons minced flat-leaf parsley

Combine all of the ingredients for the marinade in a glass measure. Place the chicken pieces in a sealable plastic bag and pour the marinade over. Refrigerate for 2 to 3 hours, turning the bag once.

Remove the chicken pieces from the marinade; reserve the marinade. Sprinkle the chicken lightly with salt and black pepper.

Pour a cup of the broth into the marinade bag, and transfer that mixture to a 1-quart glass measure. Add the remaining 3 cups broth. Sprinkle the crumbled saffron over the broth and bring to a boil in a microwave oven, 5 to 10 minutes, depending on the oven's wattage. Keep the mixture hot.

Preheat the oven to 400°F (gas) or 450°F (electric).

Heat the oil in a 15-inch paella pan over medium-high heat. Add the chicken and sauté, turning once, for about 5 minutes total (it should not be fully cooked). Remove the chicken from the pan and keep warm. Scatter the chorizo coins in the pan and stir-fry for 2 minutes. Add the onion and bell peppers to the pan and sauté until the vegetables are slightly softened. Stir in the tomatoes and cook for another 2 minutes.

Add the rice and stir to coat well. Pour in all of the hot broth and bring to a boil. Continue boiling, stirring and rotating the pan occasionally, until the mixture is no longer soupy but sufficient liquid remains to continue cooking the rice, about 4 minutes.

Discard the bay leaves and arrange the chicken pieces over the rice. Transfer to the oven and cook, uncovered, until the rice is almost al dente, 10 to 13 minutes in a gas oven, 15 to 20 in an electric oven. Remove the pan from the oven, cover it with a lid or heavy-duty aluminum foil, and let the paella sit 5 to 10 minutes, until the rice is cooked to taste. It should be nice and chewy.

4 garlic cloves, pressed

2 teaspoons sweet Spanish smoked paprika

Kosher salt

3 to 3½ pounds chicken legs and thighs, cut into 1½-to 2-inch pieces

4 cups low-sodium chicken broth

⅛ teaspoon crumbled saffron threads

3 tablespoons olive oil

9½-ounces Spanish hot or sweet dried chorizo (Palacios), sliced into ¼-inch coins

1 medium onion, finely chopped

1 medium green bell pepper, seeded and chopped into ¼-inch dice

1 medium red bell pepper, seeded and chopped into ¼-inch dice

One 14-ounce can diced tomatoes, preferably Muir Glen, with some of their juices

2 cups Spanish short-grain rice, preferably Valencia or Arroz Bomba

Chicken Cacciatore

Yield: 3 servings

This is a stepped-up approach to a classic recipe, incorporating mushrooms, olives, and lots of red and green bell peppers. I also use all chicken thighs, because they withstand all that cooking with equanimity, whereas white meat would dry out. If you must use breasts, use them on the bone with the skin.

1 cup olive oil

1 medium carrot, grated

2 red bell peppers, seeded and sliced

2 green bell peppers, seeded and sliced

1 large onion, thickly sliced

2 celery stalks, peeled and sliced diagonally into 2-inch pieces

One 15-ounce can tomato sauce

Salt

Freshly ground black pepper

3 pounds chicken thighs, bone in, skin on

Garlic powder

2 tablespoons unsalted butter

8 ounces smallish button mushrooms, quartered

1 teaspoon fresh thyme leaves, or ½ teaspoon dried thyme (optional)

½ cup pitted Kalamata olives, chopped

Preheat the oven to 400°F.

Heat ½ cup of the oil in a large skillet over medium heat. Add the grated carrot, bell peppers, onion, and celery and stir until the vegetables barely soften, about 5 minutes. Stir in the tomato sauce, salt, black pepper, and the parsley and basil. Let this simmer for 15 minutes.

Meanwhile, in a large roasting pan, coat the chicken with the remaining ½ cup oil. Season with salt, pepper, and garlic powder to taste. Roast the chicken in the preheated oven for 45 minutes. Pour the vegetable mixture over the chicken and bake, stirring often, for 30 minutes more.

Ten minutes before serving, melt the butter in a roomy skillet over medium heat. When foaming, toss in the quartered mushrooms and season with salt and black pepper. Brown the mushrooms without moving the skillet for 3 minutes, then stir and let sear, undisturbed, for 3 minutes. Turn off the heat, but keep the mushrooms warm. Scatter with the thyme leaves if using.

Divide the chicken and sauce among 2 to 3 plates. Scatter with the mushrooms and the chopped olives. Serve at once.

Bourbon Chicken Milanese

Yield: 3 to 4 servings

A very simple and very pleasing chicken dish. You can use chicken breast meat, but watch it—it dries out if it's overcooked.

In a large glass measure, combine the soy sauce, Kitchen Bouquet, bourbon, brown sugar, garlic, and ginger and whisk until the brown sugar has dissolved.

Slice the thigh meat into bite-size pieces. Place in a sealable plastic bag and pour the marinade over. Marinate overnight, refrigerated, turning the bag once or twice.

Preheat the oven to 400°F.

Drain the chicken and reserve the marinade. Arrange the chicken pieces in a single layer on an aluminum foil–lined baking sheet. Roast the chicken until browned, 15 to 20 minutes.

Meanwhile, bring the marinade to a full boil and let it bubble away for 5 to 6 minutes. Add the chicken, stir to coat, and serve with rice.

½ cup soy sauce

2 teaspoons Kitchen Bouquet

½ cup bourbon

½ cup packed dark brown sugar

3 garlic cloves, pressed

One 1-inch piece fresh ginger, peeled and grated

1½ pounds boneless, skinless chicken thighs

Denver had been trying out her cooking skills on her boyfriend, the very handsome Bobby Santangelo Stanislopoulos.
"Wow!" Bobby exclaimed, finishing off his plate of Bourbon Chicken Milanese. "You did good."
Denver nodded. "Lucky's recipe—but don't get used to home-cooked meals, I'm an assistant D.A., not a cook!"

Grilled Lime Chicken with Fontina Cheese and Dried Chile Sauce

Yield: 4 servings

MARINADE

2 garlic cloves

⅓ cup freshly squeezed lime juice (about 3 heavy limes)

2 teaspoons peeled and grated fresh ginger

¼ cup dry white vermouth

¼ cup soy sauce

3 tablespoons canola oil, plus additional for brushing the grill

1 tablespoon light brown sugar

1 teaspoon ground turmeric

½ teaspoon ground cinnamon

½ teaspoon ground mace

1 tablespoon chopped fresh oregano leaves

2 heaping teaspoons chopped fresh rosemary leaves

1 teaspoon cayenne pepper

DRIED CHILE SAUCE

(about 1½ cups)

2 dried ancho chiles, stemmed, seeded, torn into pieces

If you can't get fresh oregano, use 1 tablespoon of chopped fresh thyme leaves. The chicken needs to marinate overnight, so plan accordingly.

For the marinade: Press the garlic into a 1-quart glass measure and add the lime juice. Whisk in the ginger, vermouth, soy sauce, oil, sugar, turmeric, cinnamon, mace, oregano, rosemary, and cayenne. Place the chicken in a sealable plastic bag and pour the marinade over. Press the air out of the bag and massage the marinade into the chicken for a few minutes. Refrigerate the chicken overnight, turning the bag occasionally.

For the chile sauce: Place chiles in a 1-quart glass measure, cover them with the chicken stock, and bring to a boil in a microwave oven. (Time will vary according to the microwave oven's wattage.) Let the chiles stand until they're very soft, about 40 minutes. Drain them, reserving ½ cup of the soaking liquid.

Using an immersion blender, purée the chiles in the glass measure with ¼ cup of the soaking liquid and the lime juice. Add the crème fraîche, brown sugar, oregano, rosemary, cumin, coriander, and five-spice powder and purée with the immersion blender until smooth. Season to taste with salt and pepper. If the sauce seems too thick, add a little more of the soaking liquid. Refrigerate, covered, until ready to use, then microwave the sauce, stirring every 30 seconds, until hot.

For the chicken: Bring a charcoal fire to high heat. Brush the grate lightly with canola oil. Remove the chicken breasts from the marinade. Grill the chicken until just cooked through, turning occasionally, about 8 minutes. Quickly divide the fontina cheese among the breasts, cover the grill, and grill until the cheese melts, about 1½ minutes.

Transfer the chicken to individual serving plates. Serve with the Dried Chile Sauce on the side, with ramekins of chopped scallions for scattering on the chicken after it's coated with the sauce.

Oh yes, this is the perfect dish for an evening at home. Delicious. A feast for two. Add music by R. Kelly, a refreshing Bellini, mood lighting, and you're all set to go.

1 dried New Mexican chile, stemmed, seeded, torn into pieces

2 dried chipotle chiles (or more if you want more heat), stemmed, seeded, torn into pieces

2 cups chicken stock (low-sodium if canned)

2 tablespoons freshly squeezed lime juice

½ cup crème fraîche

2 tablespoons dark brown sugar

1 tablespoon chopped fresh oregano

1 teaspoon chopped fresh rosemary

½ teaspoon ground cumin

½ teaspoon ground coriander

1 teaspoon Chinese five-spice powder

Kosher salt

Freshly ground black pepper

CHICKEN
4 boneless, skinless chicken breast halves

1 cup grated fontina cheese, or other melting cheese, such as Monterey Jack

¼ cup chopped scallions

Dried Chile Sauce

¼ cup chopped scallions

Chicken Breasts with Roasted Lemon, Green Olive, and Capers

Yield: 2 to 4 servings

This is intensely delicious and very fast, if you have everything on hand.

To roast the lemon slices, preheat the oven to 325°F. Line a baking sheet with parchment paper. Arrange the lemon slices in a single layer on the parchment paper. Brush the slices with olive oil and sprinkle lightly with salt. Roast until slightly dry and beginning to brown around the edges, about 25 minutes. Set aside.

Sprinkle the chicken with salt and pepper. Dredge the chicken in flour to coat on both sides, shaking off the excess. Heat the olive oil in a large heavy-bottomed skillet over high heat. Add the chicken and cook until golden brown, about 3 minutes per side. Transfer the chicken to a plate and keep warm.

Add the chicken broth, olives, capers, vermouth, cinnamon, mace, and mustard to the skillet and bring to a boil, scraping up the browned bits from the bottom. Boil for about 5 minutes, or until the liquid has reduced to a syrup consistency. Stir in the butter and roasted lemon slices, and return the chicken breasts to the sauce. Simmer just until chicken is cooked through, about 2 minutes.

Serve sprinkled with chopped cilantro and a grind or two of black pepper. Garnish with additional olives and lemon wedges.

16 thin lemon slices, about ⅛ inch thick, from 2 lemons (Use a mandoline if you've got one, and pick out any seeds.)

⅓ cup olive oil, plus more, for anointing the lemon slices

Kosher salt

Freshly ground black pepper

4 large boneless, skinless chicken breast halves

All-purpose flour

½ cup pitted and chopped green Sicilian olives, or other brine-cured green olives

2 tablespoons capers, preferably salt-packed, thoroughly rinsed and drained

2 tablespoons white wine or dry French vermouth

½ teaspoon ground cinnamon

½ teaspoon ground mace

½ teaspoon dry mustard

4 tablespoons (½ stick) unsalted butter, cut into tablespoon-size pieces

Chopped fresh cilantro, for garnish

Coq au Vin

Yield: 4 servings

The chicken legs really should marinate overnight, so plan accordingly.

2 medium carrots, sliced crosswise

2 onions, coarsely chopped

3 celery stalks, coarsely chopped

6 large fresh thyme sprigs

2 bay leaves

One 750-ml bottle dry red wine

6 whole chicken legs with thighs and drumsticks attached

1½ cups frozen pearl onions

5 tablespoons (½ stick plus 1 tablespoon) unsalted butter, at room temperature

12 ounces large mushrooms, quartered

5 thick bacon slices, chopped

1½ cups Port wine

2 tablespoons Wondra flour

Place the carrots, onions, celery, thyme, bay leaves, and wine in a large sealable plastic freezer bag. Add the chicken and submerge it completely. Seal the bag and chill in the refrigerator for at least 4 hours, or preferably overnight.

Meanwhile, thaw the pearl onions in the refrigerator, or microwave them when you're ready to proceed.

Melt 3 tablespoons of the butter in a large, deep, heavy-bottomed skillet over medium-high heat. Add the thawed pearl onions and the quartered mushrooms and sauté together until the mushrooms are tender, about 10 minutes. Transfer the mushroom mixture to a bowl.

Add the chopped bacon to the same skillet and sauté until browned and crisp. Transfer the bacon to paper towels to drain and reserve 2 to 3 tablespoons of the bacon fat in the skillet. Turn off the burner while you ready the chicken.

Using a slotted spoon, transfer the chicken from the marinade to a strainer; reserve the marinade and the vegetables. Pat the chicken dry with paper towels and season with salt and pepper. Return the skillet with the bacon fat to medium-high heat. Carefully add the chicken and sauté until the skin is good and brown, turning once, about 10 minutes.

Pour the marinade and the vegetables over the chicken and bring to a boil. Reduce the heat and simmer the chicken, uncovered, until it is very tender, about 1 hour and 15 minutes.

Place a large strainer over a large bowl. Strain the chicken, vegetables, and cooking liquid into the bowl. Transfer the chicken to another bowl; discard the vegetables in the strainer.

Return the liquid to the skillet, add the Port wine, and bring to a boil.

In a small bowl, using a fork, combine the flour with the remaining 2 tablespoons butter. Whisk the butter mixture into the cooking liquid. Boil over medium heat until the sauce thickens and has slightly reduced, about 15 minutes.

Return the chicken to the pot. Add the pearl onions, mushrooms, and bacon to the chicken and wine mixture. Simmer until heated through and the flavors have blended, stirring and turning the chicken occasionally, about 10 minutes. Serve the chicken drizzled with the sauce.

Roasted Sage Sausages and Grapes

Yield: 2 servings

This is pretty much ready in about half an hour, making it a great fast dish for two. It can easily be doubled or tripled.

1 pound sage country sausages or breakfast sausages, thawed if frozen

1 pound green and/or red seedless grapes

3 tablespoons unsalted butter

⅛ cup balsamic vinegar (white, if you can get it)

Preheat the oven to 500°F.

In a saucepan large enough to hold the sausages in a single layer, braise the sausages in an inch of simmering water for 7 minutes.

Put the butter in a large (2½-quart) gratin dish and melt the butter in the oven. Add the grapes and toss to coat. Transfer the sausages with tongs to the gratin dish and push them down into the grapes.

Roast, turning the sausages once, for about 15 minutes, or until the grapes are soft and the sausages are lightly browned. Remove from the oven, drizzle the balsamic vinegar over the mixture, and stir a bit. Return the dish to the oven and continue to roast for 5 minutes, or until the juices reduce.

New potatoes roasted in a bit of goose fat are a great complement to this dish.

Duck Burgers with Onion Marmalade

Yield: 2 burgers

A succulent and relatively rapid duck preparation, the sweetish onion marmalade really gooses up the duck. Panko are now widely available in supermarkets.

Cut the duck breast into 1-inch cubes, keeping the fat but discarding the skin. If using duck legs, debone them and remove the skin, but keep the fat. You should have about 2 ounces of fat, cubed.

Pulse the parsley in a food processor and chop finely. Add the garlic and pulse to mince. Add the duck meat and fat and pulse until finely and uniformly chopped, 30 to 35 quick pulses. Transfer the duck mixture to a bowl and work in the panko, salt, and pepper. Form into 2 patties and refrigerate, covered with waxed paper.

Preheat a broiler or grill until very hot.

Melt the duck fat in a cast-iron skillet set over medium-low heat, add the onions, and sauté until tender and golden, about 20 minutes. Stir in the mustard and wine and season with salt and pepper.

Grill or broil the patties until medium rare, 2 to 3 minutes per side, depending on the heat. Toast the buns, reheat the onions, and serve the burgers in the buns topped with a good heap of onions.

1 large magret duck breast (about 1 pound) or 2 large duck legs (about 1 pound total)

1 tablespoon flat-leaf parsley

1 garlic clove, peeled

¼ cup panko

Kosher salt

Freshly ground black pepper

1 tablespoon duck fat or olive oil

1 large Vidalia onion, thinly sliced

1½ tablespoons smooth Dijon mustard

2 tablespoons dry red wine, or 1 tablespoon dry white vermouth and 1 tablespoon red wine vinegar

2 brioche buns

The young stud sitting opposite Venus in the expensive restaurant stared at the menu as if it was written in a foreign language.

"Problem?" Venus asked, thinking how handsome he looked in the Dolce & Gabbana jacket she'd recently bought him.

"Naw," he answered, his strong New York accent somewhat grating. "It's just that . . ."

"What?"

"Who the hell has friggin' duck with marmalade? It's some kinda crazy."

Venus smiled. So sweet. So unsophisticated. So sexy.

"Calm down," she said soothingly. "I'm sure if we ask they can make you a burger."

"Ya think?"

"Yes. I think that for me they'll do anything."

Lucky's Get-You-Going Turkey

Yield: at least 10 servings, with leftovers

The mustard rub really perks up the turkey flavors, and by placing it under the skin, you'll get extra-crispy skin. Be sure to marinate overnight as instructed. The day after roasting, this makes the best turkey sandwiches I've ever had.

2 garlic cloves, peeled

½ cup flat-leaf parsley leaves

2 tablespoons fresh rosemary leaves

1 tablespoon fresh thyme leaves

1 tablespoon fresh sage leaves

1 cup smooth Dijon mustard

¾ cup olive oil

Zest and juice of 1 large lemon

¼ cup low-sodium soy sauce

1 teaspoon freshly ground black pepper

One 15- to 16-pound fresh turkey

2 cups low-sodium chicken broth

Coarsely chop the garlic, parsley, rosemary, thyme, and sage in a food processor. Add the mustard, olive oil, lemon zest and juice, soy sauce, and pepper and coarsely purée. Reserve ½ cup of the mixture in a measuring cup.

Rinse the turkey inside and out under cool running water, then pat it completely dry with paper towels. Snip off the wing tips with a pair of poultry shears. Gently slide your hand under the skin of the breast, legs, and thighs and loosen the skin from the flesh. With the same hand, spread 1 cup of the mustard mixture under the skin and over the meat of the breast, legs, and thighs. Spread the remaining mustard mixture inside the bird's cavity.

Place the turkey on a rack set in a large roasting pan. Place the reserved ½ cup mustard mixture alongside. Slide everything into an enormous plastic bag, seal the bag, and refrigerate the turkey for at least 1 day and up to 2 days.

Position a rack in the bottom third of the oven. Preheat to 325°F.

Spread the reserved ½ cup mustard mixture all over the turkey. Roast the turkey for 2 hours. Baste with ½ cup of the broth.

Continue to roast until the turkey is nicely browned, basting frequently with the remaining 1½ cups broth and pan juices, about 1½ hours longer. A thermometer inserted in thickest part of the thigh should register 168°F. Cover the bird loosely with foil if you think it's browning too quickly.

Transfer the turkey to a serving platter. Tent it loosely with foil, and let it rest 30 minutes before carving. The pan juices will make a lovely gravy base.

Pork Chops Milanese

Yield: 2 servings

Here's a twist on the more traditional veal chops Milanese. For me the pork has more flavor. It's a great romantic dinner for two, but the recipe can easily be doubled.

Season both sides of the chops generously with salt and pepper. Place a chop between two sheets of plastic wrap and pound it mercilessly with a mallet until it's flattened into a semicircle of pork ⅛ inch thick. Repeat with the other chop.

Line up 3 shallow, wide bowls on the countertop. Put the flour in the first bowl, the beaten eggs in the second, and stir together the panko, the grated Parmigiano-Reggiano, ½ teaspoon salt and ¼ teaspoon pepper, and the rosemary in the third. Place a wire rack over a baking sheet. Dip each cutlet in the flour, shaking off any excess, then dip in the eggs, and finally in the crumb mixture, patting both sides to make sure they're well coated. Set the coated cutlets on the rack over the baking sheet. When the cutlets are coated, refrigerate for 30 minutes, or for up to 6 hours.

Add enough olive oil to a large skillet to cover the bottom by ¼ inch. Heat over medium-high heat until the oil starts to shimmer. Add 1 pork cutlet (or both if they fit), and cook until golden brown, 1½ to 2 minutes per side. Transfer to paper towels to drain. Repeat to cook the remaining cutlet.

While the cutlets are cooking, in a bowl quickly toss the arugula with the tomato halves, olive oil, and lemon juice.

Serve the cutlets piping hot, topped with the arugula salad and Parmigiano-Reggiano shavings, with lemon wedges on the side.

Two boneless pork loin chops (about 6 ounces each)

Kosher salt

Freshly ground black pepper

¼ cup all-purpose flour

2 large eggs, beaten

1½ cups panko (Japanese-style bread crumbs)

½ cup freshly grated Parmigiano-Reggiano cheese

½ teaspoon finely chopped fresh rosemary

½ cup (or more) extra-virgin olive oil

2 cups baby arugula, washed and dried, at room temperature

16 pear or cherry tomatoes, halved

¼ cup extra-virgin olive oil

Juice of 1 large lemon

Parmigiano-Reggiano shavings, for garnish

Pork Chops Saltimbocca with Sautéed Spinach

Yield: 2 servings

Again, this is more traditionally prepared with veal chops, and without spinach, but I think this is tastier and certainly less expensive.

Two 1-inch-thick, center-cut rib pork chops

2 fresh sage leaves, finely chopped

2 thin slices fontina cheese

2 thin slices prosciutto

2 tablespoons olive oil

1 large garlic clove, pressed

One 10-ounce bag fresh spinach, stems discarded

2 tablespoons unsalted butter, cut into pieces

1 tablespoon freshly squeezed lemon juice

Position a rack in the middle of the oven and preheat the oven to 450°F.

Cut a deep, wide pocket in each pork chop. Sprinkle half the sage into each pocket and stuff each pocket with the cheese and prosciutto. Pat the chops dry and season with ¼ teaspoon each of salt and pepper.

Heat 1 tablespoon of the oil in a 12-inch, cast-iron skillet over medium-high heat until it shimmers. Add the chops and cook until undersides are golden, about 2 minutes. Turn the chops, transfer the skillet to the hot oven to finish the cooking, 4 to 5 minutes, or until cooked through.

While the chops finish cooking, heat the remaining 1 tablespoon oil in a 5-quart pot over medium heat until it shimmers. Add the garlic and sauté for about 30 seconds. Add the spinach and cook, covered, stirring occasionally, until wilted, about 30 minutes. Season with salt.

Transfer the chops to plates. Add the butter and lemon juice to the hot skillet, stirring and scraping up the browned bits on the bottom, then pour the pan sauce over the pork. Serve with the spinach.

Pork Tenderloin with Honey-Mustard Sauce

Yield: 4 servings

Whisk together the beer, mustard, honey, olive oil, rosemary, and garlic. Place the pork tenderloins in a sealable plastic bag and pour the marinade over them. Massage the marinade into the tenderloins and marinate overnight, refrigerated, turning the bag every so often.

Preheat the oven to 350°F. Place the tenderloins on a roasting rack set on a rimmed baking sheet; reserve the marinade. Roast until a meat thermometer registers 150°F, about 55 minutes. Remove from the oven and let the meat rest, loosely tented with aluminum foil, for 15 minutes.

Meanwhile, strain the marinade into a heavy-bottomed, medium saucepan. Add the cream and any juices from the roasting pan. Bring the mixture to a boil, then lower the heat and simmer for 15 minutes. (Watch out—the mixture will tend to boil over for the first 5 minutes or so.) Season the reduced sauce with salt and pepper to taste.

Cut the tenderloin into 1-inch slices and serve over rice with the sauce drizzled on top.

¾ cup beer (not dark)

½ cup smooth Dijon mustard

6 tablespoons honey

¼ cup olive oil

2 tablespoons chopped fresh rosemary

3 garlic cloves, pressed

2 pork tenderloins (about 1½ to 2 pounds)

½ cup heavy cream

Kosher salt

Freshly ground black pepper

Steamed rice, for serving

Food or sex? Sometimes that's the dilemma that Venus finds herself facing. She loves to eat, but she also realizes that her figure is her fortune so therefore she cannot overindulge.

Dinner with yet another boy toy solves the problem. Vito also loves to eat. He loves sex, too, and he has a vicarious appetite for both activities. So before retiring for the night, Venus decides she will treat Vito to a culinary feast. Pork Tenderloin with Honey-Mustard Sauce. Delicious. Light. Sexy.

And after . . . fully satisfied . . . there will be a luxurious relax before dessert. And Venus always makes sure that dessert is something special. . . .

Pulled Pork Tacos

Yield: 16 tacos

Once the pork shoulder is braised in the oven, this dish comes together rapidly and tastes great.

Preheat the oven to 350°F. Place the pork in a 3-quart (or larger) Dutch oven. Combine the tomatoes, onion, apple juice, lime juice, garlic, chili powder, and salt in a medium bowl. Pour the mixture over the pork and cover. Bake the pork for 3 to 3½ hours until very tender.

Remove the pork from the Dutch oven and cool slightly. Remove any fat or bones and shred the pork with a fork. Strain the tomato-onion mixture and return the tomatoes and onions to the Dutch oven. Add the shredded pork to the sauce in the Dutch oven and mix well.

Watchfully toast each tortilla on both sides over open gas flames or under a hot broiler.

Stack the tortillas on a plate and steam them in a microwave, until soft and pliable, 1 to 2 minutes. Place ¼ cup of the shredded meat on each tortilla. Top each taco with avocado slices, tomatillo salsa, and a dollop of sour cream. Serve with minced jalapeños and hot sauce on the side.

3 pounds pork shoulder, bone in

One 14-ounce can organic diced tomatoes with mild green chilies (or use regular diced tomatoes and a separate small can of mild green chilies)

1 cup chopped onion

½ cup apple juice

2 tablespoons freshly squeezed lime juice

2 garlic cloves, minced

2 teaspoons chili powder

½ teaspoon kosher salt

Sixteen 6-inch corn tortillas

4 ripe avocados, peeled, pitted, and sliced

1 cup tomatillo salsa (or salsa verde)

1 cup sour cream

Minced jalapeños, for serving

Tabasco sauce, for serving

Sweet and Spicy Spareribs

Yield: 4 to 6 servings

I'm crazy about spareribs. Nothing like a down-and-dirty barbecue to have fun.

This recipe also works well with baby back ribs, which take less time to cook through—about a half hour. The internal temperature of the cooked ribs should be the same—165° to 175°F.

2 cups dry sherry

2 pounds brown sugar

¾ cup apple cider vinegar

2 tablespoons balsamic vinegar

2 tablespoons molasses

2 cups soy sauce

¾ cup ketchup

1 tablespoon ground ginger

6 garlic cloves, minced or pressed

1 tablespoon Tabasco sauce, or more as needed

1 lemon

4 racks spareribs (about 10 pounds)

In a large saucepan, combine the sherry, brown sugar, apple cider vinegar, balsamic, molasses, soy sauce, ketchup, ginger, garlic, and Tabasco to taste. Whisk together thoroughly, then squeeze the lemon, throw away the seeds, and toss the juice and the lemon into the marinade. Bring the mixture to a boil, stirring often, then remove it from the heat and let cool.

Slather the ribs with the sauce, transfer to a large sealable plastic bag, and marinate in the refrigerator for 24 hours.

Preheat the broiler. Drain the ribs and reserve the marinade. Broil the ribs until golden brown, about 3 minutes per side. Meanwhile, bring the marinade to a boil and simmer for 10 to 15 minutes, to thicken into a glaze.

Preheat the oven to 425°F. Place the ribs on a rack (or two) and place in a roasting pan (or two). Brush on some of the glaze, and roast the ribs for 45 minutes. Turn them, brush on more of the glaze, and roast the ribs for 30 minutes per pound. The ribs are done when the internal temperature registers 165° to 175°F.

Let the ribs rest for 10 minutes, then separate them with a carving knife, brush them with additional glaze, and serve.

Lucky's Luscious Meatballs

Yield: about 20 meatballs

The large quantity of chopped parsley—1 cup!—certainly gives the meatballs a toothsome herbal quality.

SEASONED STOCK
½ cup chicken stock

½ large sweet onion, such as Vidalia, finely chopped

3 to 4 garlic cloves, minced

1 cup flat-leaf parsley leaves, loosely packed, finely chopped

MEATBALLS
¾ pound ground beef (chuck about 80% lean)

¾ pound ground pork

½ cup plain dry bread crumbs

4 large eggs, plus 2 egg yolks

2 large onions chopped

½ cup grated Parmigiano-Reggiano cheese

2 or 3 pinches crushed red pepper flakes

2 or 3 pinches Kosher salt

Extra-virgin olive oil, for frying

2 to 3 cups favorite marinara sauce

For the seasoned stock: Place all the ingredients in a mini food processor and purée. Set aside.

For the meatballs: Combine the ground meats, dry bread crumbs, eggs, egg yolks, onions, cheese, red pepper flakes, salt, and the puréed stock mixture in a large bowl and mix lightly with your hands just until the mixture is uniform; try not to overmix.

Form the mixture into 20 balls about the size of golf balls. Line them up on a sheet of waxed paper. Heat the marinara sauce in a roomy saucepan. Keep at a simmer.

In a large skillet over medium-high heat, heat about ½ inch of olive oil. Without crowding the skillet, brown the meatballs for about 10 minutes, turning them once. When they are browned to your liking, remove the meatballs from the oil using a slotted spoon and submerge them in the lightly bubbling marinara sauce. Simmer for 30 minutes, or just until the meatballs are cooked through and tender. Serve the meatballs with crusty garlic bread slices, or over spaghetti.

Meatballs. A big Santangelo favorite. Perfect to accompany any kind of pasta, good on their own, and especially delicious when eaten cold for breakfast.

"Mornin'," Max, Lucky's teenage daughter said, sauntering onto the terrace of their Malibu beach house.

Lucky gave her a pointed look. "Late night?" she questioned.

"Kinda," Max said, grinning.

Lucky could see the fire in her daughter's eyes. Max was a wild child, just like she'd been, and she knew that above all else she had to let her run free.

"You missed spaghetti and meatballs for dinner last night," Lucky remarked.

"No!" Max said, pulling a face.

"Yes."

"Any leftovers?"

"Check it out, but I doubt it. Lennie went on a late-night fridge raid last night, so I guess you're probably out of luck."

"Bummer!" Max exclaimed. And there and then she decided she had to learn how to cook, or at least know how to make Lucky's Luscious Meatballs.

The Best Hamburger in Town!

Yield: 8 big burgers

Hamburgers are at an all-time high in popularity, and for good reasons: they're a meal in themselves, they're portable, and this rendition is especially tangy and delicious.

Do not press down on the burgers with a spatula while they're cooking—you'll push out all the good juices. And keep in mind that chuck beef has just the right amount of fat to provide you with juicy, tender burgers. This recipe is easily halved.

In a large bowl, combine the beef, ketchup, garlic, parsley, and salt and pepper to taste and mix well. Fashion into 10-ounce patties.

Preheat a cast-iron skillet over high heat or take the patties outside to the grill. Cook the patties, turning once, for 4 minutes per side for medium-rare. Tuck each burger into a lightly toasted, buttered bun and serve with your preferred condiments. Or try serving the burgers with the Blender Hollandaise Sauce (page 131).

5 pounds ground top rib or chuck beef (about 15 percent fat)

1 pint Heinz ketchup

2 garlic cloves, pressed or finely minced

3 tablespoons finely chopped flat-leaf parsley

Kosher salt

Freshly ground black pepper

8 potato hamburger buns, split, toasted, and buttered

Bobby Santangelo Stanislopoulos—tall, dark, and cool, with a swagger women can't resist, and a wicked sense of humor. Like most men, the one thing Bobby cannot resist is a big fat juicy burger—and to make sure, when the barbecue is flying, so is Bobby. He makes the best burger in town!

Peppered Beef Stroganoff

Yield: 3 to 4 servings

Don't be stingy with the black pepper here. This dish should sting and then soothe.

1 tablespoon coarsely ground black pepper, or more as desired

Kosher salt

Eight 8-ounce beef tenderloin steaks

3 tablespoons olive oil

8 ounces shiitake mushrooms, stemmed and halved or quartered if large

1¼ cups beef broth

1 tablespoon cognac or brandy

½ cup heavy cream

1 tablespoon Dijon mustard

One 8-ounce package wide egg noodles

2 tablespoons chopped flat-leaf parsley

Sprinkle the pepper and salt over both sides of the steaks, pressing to make the pepper adhere. Heat 1 tablespoon of the oil in a large skillet over medium-high heat. Add the steaks and cook to the desired doneness, 2 to 3 minutes per side for rare. Transfer the beef to a plate and tent loosely with aluminum foil.

Add 1 tablespoon of the oil to the same skillet. Add the mushrooms and sauté until browned, about 4 minutes. Add the broth and cognac and boil for 2 minutes. Add the cream and boil until slightly thickened, about 3 minutes. Whisk in the mustard.

Meanwhile, cook the noodles in a pot of boiling salted water until just tender but still firm to the bite, stirring occasionally. Drain. Return to the pot and toss with the parsley and the remaining 1 tablespoon oil. Season with salt and pepper and divide among warm plates.

Slice the steaks and arrange over the noodles. Spoon the sauce over the top.

To flambé: At the table, pour a tablespoon of cognac or brandy from a measuring cup over each plate. Warn your guests to lean back, then carefully ignite the cognac with a long match or long butane candle lighter.

Gino and Lucky. Two of a kind. Father and daughter. A tempestuous relationship with many ups and downs. When Gino married his wild-child daughter off at sixteen to a senator's son she vowed to always hate her father. But when Gino was forced out of the country on a tax exile, and Lucky took over the family business, things changed. Now Gino has mellowed and Lucky is all powerful.

The Russian Tea Room in New York. A red leather booth for two. The Santangelos. Gino and Lucky.

Gino: "You know how many years I bin comin' here?"

Lucky: "Too many."

Gino: "Ah, she knows me so well."

Lucky: "I sure do."

Gino: "You do, cause you're just like me."

Lucky: "You think?"

Gino: "I know."

Lucky: "Order your special beef stroganoff, old man, while I sip a White Russian."

Gino: "Kiddo, we're two of a kind."

Lucky nodded. She'd reached a stage in life where she was proud to be Gino's daughter.

Lucky's Kick-Ass Chili

Yield: 4 servings

2 ancho chiles, lightly toasted in a dry skillet

2 guajillo chiles, lightly toasted in a dry skillet

2 to 3 canned chipotle chiles in adobo

2 tablespoons corn oil

1 medium white onion, chopped

2 garlic cloves, pressed

1¼ pounds ground chuck

One 14-ounce can diced tomatoes, preferably Muir Glen

½ ounce unsweetened chocolate, grated

1 teaspoon freshly ground black pepper

¼ teaspoon, of each: ground cumin, ground turmeric, ground allspice, ground cinnamon, ground cloves, ground coriander, ground cardamom

½ teaspoon kosher salt

16-ounce can red kidney beans

9 ounces spaghetti

2 tablespoons unsalted butter

1 pound cheddar cheese, finely shredded

Sour cream, for serving

Chopped white onion or scallions

Minced jalapeños

The majority of the ingredients called for in this intensely delicious chili are in most well-stocked pantries.

Place the toasted ancho and guajillo chiles in a medium bowl and cover with 1 cup of boiling water. Nest a smaller bowl over the chiles to keep them immersed. Let stand for 30 minutes. Strain and reserve the water. Stem and seed the chiles and purée them in a food processor with ¾ cup of the reserved, strained water and the canned chipotles.

In a 3-quart Dutch oven, heat the oil over medium heat. Add the chopped onion and garlic and sauté, stirring occasionally, for 5 minutes. Add the beef and brown, stirring to keep it loose. Drain any fat from the pan. Add the puréed chiles and the tomatoes and bring the mixture to a boil. Add the chocolate, spices, and salt. Cover, reduce the heat, and simmer for 30 minutes, stirring occasionally. The chili will thicken as it cooks.

Drain and rinse the kidney beans and stir them into the chili. Allow the chili to rest at least 30 minutes in a covered pan at room temperature, then reheat.

Meanwhile, cook the spaghetti until just tender. Drain and toss with the butter.

To make each plate, start with a layer of spaghetti; top it with the hot chili, and pat on some cheese so the chili's heat can begin to melt it. Serve immediately with sour cream, chopped onions, and minced jalapeños.

Max is into chili cookouts on the beach. It's her one specialty, and all her friends are wild for it. She usually prepares it in the family kitchen, then with the help of her two best friends, Cookie and Harry, they lug everything down to the sand, where they light a fire.

It's a feast—with plenty of Red Bull and music courtesy of Lady Gaga and Adam Levine.

Max, like her mom, knows how to have a good time!

Rococo Meat loaf

Yield: about 6 servings

Nearly every cook has his or her very own meat loaf recipe. Mine has a lot of "traditional" meat loaf touches. It's very rich, thanks to all that cheese, and, like any meat loaf worth its ground beef, it does well hot, cold, or in between. The texture is unusually supple, fluffy, and tender, especially if you don't manhandle the meat mix before baking it. For a smokier and spicier loaf, finely chop and add 2 to 3 minced, canned chipotle peppers in adobo to the meat mixture. Start this a good two hours before serving. Don't let this loaf ooze too little or too much, and do use a meat thermometer.

1 cup fresh bread crumbs (you may need somewhat more)

4 tablespoons (½ stick) unsalted butter

3 garlic cloves

4 scallions, white and light green parts only, halved lengthwise and sliced into 1½-inch lengths

2 large or 3 medium onions, peeled and quartered

1 medium red bell pepper, quartered, stemmed, and seeded

2 large eggs, beaten

⅓ cup low-sodium beef broth

1 tablespoon Worcestershire sauce

Tabasco sauce (vaguely optional)

1 tablespoon soy sauce

First, if you need to, make the fresh bread crumbs in the work bowl of your food processor by pulsing torn chunks of bread. (You might as well make plenty of extra crumbs and freeze them in a sealed plastic bag. They keep for several months.) Rinse out the work bowl.

In a large skillet, melt the butter over medium-low heat.

Pulse the garlic, scallions, onions, and bell pepper in the bowl of a food processor, in the order in which they are listed, until minced, but not mushy. The onion mixture will be fairly wet. Add it to the hot butter in the skillet, cover, and sweat the mixture for 5 minutes. Uncover and stir, still over medium-low heat, for 5 minutes, or until the mixture begins to brown lightly and the liquids have evaporated. Remove from the heat and let the mixture approach room temperature.

Line a shallow baking dish or rimmed baking sheet with edges at least 1 inch high with heavy-duty aluminum foil.

Position a rack in the middle of the oven. Preheat the oven to 350°F.

In a medium bowl, whisk together the eggs, beef broth, Worcestershire sauce, hot sauce, and soy sauce until well blended.

In a large bowl, lightly combine the ground beef, pork, veal, sausage, cheese, and bread crumbs with your squeaky clean hands. Don't overmix—use a light touch. Then add the egg mixture and the cooled onion-pepper mixture and blend well, still with a light touch. Transfer the mixture to the prepared baking dish or pan. Shape the meat into an oval mound about 2½ inches high at its thickest point and smooth the top. Using a rubber spatula, spread the ketchup evenly over the loaf, and arrange the bacon strips over the ketchup, tucking the strips under the loaf.

Bake for about 1 hour and 10 minutes, or until a thermometer inserted into the center registers 160°F. Let the loaf rest in its formidable juices for 10 minutes before slicing.

1 pound ground beef chuck (15 percent fat)

½ pound ground pork

½ pound ground veal

½ pound sweet sausage, casings removed

8 ounces Monterey Jack cheese, finely grated (about 2 cups)

½ cup ketchup

5 to 6 slices thick-cut bacon, halved crosswise

Meat loaf. A family special. Way way back, Lucky remembered her beautiful mom fixing meat loaf every Monday night. Maria, her mom, was murdered when Lucky was only five, but the bittersweet memories lingered.

Beef Tenderloin Steaks with Brandy and Mustard Sauce

Yield: 2 to 4 servings

Beef tenderloin is famously tender, but it is also famously bland, and the steaks should be served with a kick-ass sauce.

Four 1-inch-thick top loin or tenderloin steaks (about 6 ounces each)

Kosher salt

Freshly ground black pepper

2 tablespoons unsalted butter

¼ cup finely chopped shallots

1 tablespoon roughly chopped capers

½ cup low-sodium beef broth

½ cup good-quality brandy

1 tablespoon Dijon mustard

2 teaspoons Worcestershire sauce

Season both sides of the steaks with salt and pepper. In a large skillet, over medium-high heat, melt 1 tablespoon of the butter. Add the steaks and cook, turning as needed, to the desired doneness, 10 to 12 minutes for medium-rare. Reduce heat if the meat is browning too quickly.

Transfer the steaks to a platter and tent with aluminum foil to keep warm. Add the shallots and capers to the skillet and sauté briefly until the shallots are translucent. Remove the pan from the heat and add the broth and brandy, taking care not to let the liquid splatter.

Return the pan to the burner and bring to a boil over high heat, stirring with a whisk or wooden spoon to loosen any browned bits from the bottom of the pan. Boil until the liquid has reduced to ⅓ cup, 2 to 3 minutes depending on the pan size.

Whisk in the mustard and Worcestershire sauce. Then whisk in the remaining 1 tablespoon butter. Season to taste with more salt and pepper. Arrange the steaks on 2 to 4 dinner plates, spoon the sauce over the steaks, and serve.

Steak Tartare

Yield: 2 ample servings, or 6 appetizer portions

Be sure to use only the best, leanest sirloin steak. Tell your butcher that it's for steak tartare, and he'll know what to give you. I like to use those little "cocktail" pumpernickel slices that come in a foot-and-a-half sliced loaf.

Chill a roomy glass bowl in the freezer or refrigerator. In a food processor, mince the horseradish, then the parsley, and then the onion until well ground. Scrape the mixture into the chilled glass bowl.

Cut the sirloin into 4 to 5 pieces and place it in the bowl of the processor. Pulse the steak just until it barely reaches a ground-meat consistency—but not too finely. Transfer the steak to the bowl. With your impeccably clean hands, blend the horseradish-parsley-onion mixture into the beef with the Worcestershire, salt, pepper, Tabasco, olive oil, lemon juice, and egg yolks.

Toast the pumpernickel on the upper rack of a 425°F oven. Butter the pumpernickel slices, plate them, and serve the steak tartare in the glass bowl with two serving plates.

1 tablespoon-size chunk of fresh horseradish, peeled and roughly chopped

2 tablespoons flat-leaf parsley leaves

1 medium white onion, peeled and cut into chunks

1¼ pounds very lean sirloin steak

1 tablespoon Worcestershire sauce

1 teaspoon kosher salt

1 teaspoon freshly ground black pepper

2 heavy dashes Tabasco sauce

1 tablespoon extra-virgin olive oil

A good squeeze of lemon juice

4 very fresh raw large egg yolks

6 to 8 slices pumpernickel bread

Unsalted butter, at room temperature

Roast Beef Dusted with Coriander

Yield: 4 to 8 servings

Any leftovers are great in tacos or in beef stroganoff. Select a roasting pan that can withstand high stovetop heat.

Preheat the oven to 350°F.

Rub the roast with 1 tablespoon of the olive oil. In a small bowl, combine the ground coriander seeds and paprika with 2 teaspoons of the salt and 1 teaspoon of pepper. Rub the spice blend all over the meat.

Heat the remaining 1 tablespoon olive oil in a medium roasting pan over medium heat. Add the roast and brown it well on all sides, turning with tongs, about 5 minutes. Turn the roast fat side up. Transfer the roasting pan to the hot oven and roast the meat for about 35 minutes, or until an instant-read thermometer inserted in the thinner end registers 120°F for medium-rare meat. Transfer the roast to a cutting board, tent loosely with aluminum foil, and let it rest for 20 minutes.

Meanwhile, set the roasting pan over high heat. Sprinkle in the flour and cook for 2 minutes, whisking constantly. Add the stock and wine and boil, whisking, until the gravy has thickened, 2 minutes. Season with salt and pepper. Carve the roast into ¼-inch-thick slices and serve, drizzled with the gravy.

One 3¾- to 4-pound beef eye of round roast, with a layer of fat left intact on one side, at room temperature

2 tablespoons olive oil

1 tablespoon whole coriander seeds, lightly toasted and coarsely ground

1 teaspoon smoked sweet paprika

Kosher salt

Freshly ground black pepper

2 tablespoons all-purpose flour

2 cups beef stock

½ cup dry red wine, such as Rioja or Cabernet Sauvignon

Bourbon-Marinated Flank Steak

Yield: 2 to 4 servings

¼ cup bourbon

¼ cup smooth Dijon mustard, such as Maille

1 tablespoon Worcestershire sauce

1 teaspoon low-sodium soy sauce

2 teaspoons freshly squeezed lime juice

¼ teaspoon freshly ground black pepper

1½ pounds flank steak

Combine the bourbon, Dijon mustard, Worcestershire, salt, soy sauce, lime juice, and pepper in a small bowl. Place the steak in a sealable plastic bag and rub the marinade all over, coating it well. Let the steak marinate at room temperature for 30 minutes. (The steak can be marinated for up to 24 hours, covered and refrigerated.)

Once the steak has marinated, preheat a grill pan over medium-high heat or an outdoor grill. Reserve the marinade and grill the steak for 5 to 6 minutes per side for medium rare. Transfer to a cutting board and let rest for 10 to 15 minutes.

Meanwhile, in a small saucepan bring the marinade to a boil over medium-high heat. Reduce the heat, and boil the marinade until it's of a saucy consistency, 10 to 15 minutes.

Season the steak with additional salt and pepper, and slice thinly across the grain. Serve drizzled with the sauce. Consider doing a quick and dirty flambé with a little more bourbon.

What man doesn't like a big juicy steak, especially a steak steeped in bourbon. This is one of Lennie's special dishes. He likes to make it himself—usually with a couple of his guy friends over. Add a few bottles of ice-cold beer, heavy metal sounds coming from the outdoor speakers, and Lennie enjoys what he refers to as "guys' night out."

Lamb Steaks with Mushrooms

Yield: 2 servings

This is an attempt to re-create a dish I once had in Madrid. After marination, the lamb and mushrooms cook very quickly.

In a mini food processor, pulse the shallot, vinegar, olive oil, lemon juice, garlic, rosemary, paprika, salt, and pepper until the mixture is emulsified and fairly smooth. Place the lamb and the mushrooms in a sealable plastic bag and pour the marinade over them. Seal the bag and massage the marinade into the meat. Turn the bag to coat everything well, and refrigerate for 2 hours, turning the bag occasionally. The mushrooms will absorb, and later exude, a good deal of the marinade.

Heat a large, cast-iron skillet over medium-high heat until the pan is nearly smoking. Add the canola oil, then carefully lay in the steaks and mushrooms. Cook the steaks until they're done to your liking, 2 to 3 minutes per side for rare, and the mushrooms until they're nicely browned, stirring every few minutes. Pour in the cognac, ignite it carefully, and serve as soon as the flames have subsided.

1 large shallot, peeled and chopped into 8 pieces

⅛ cup red wine vinegar

¼ cup extra-virgin olive oil

2 teaspoons freshly squeezed lemon juice

1 garlic clove, pressed

1 teaspoon minced fresh rosemary

½ teaspoon Spanish smoked sweet paprika

½ teaspoon kosher salt

Freshly ground black pepper

1½ pounds lamb leg steaks, each about ¾ inch thick, or boneless leg of lamb cut into 2 steaks each about 1 inch thick

½ pound chanterelle mushrooms, trimmed

2 tablespoons canola oil

¼ cup cognac

Lamb You Can Eat with a Spoon

Yield: 6 servings

No kidding! Be sure to allow 8 hours to prepare this dish, from start to finish. This is best prepared in an oval, enameled, cast-iron Dutch oven. If peeling all that garlic dissuades you from making this, you can buy small tubs of freshly peeled garlic in better supermarkets.

One 6-pound leg of lamb on the bone (shank bone sawed off so that lamb will fit in an oval Dutch oven—no more than 12 inches long)

2 tablespoons vegetable oil

5 firm heads garlic, cloves separated and peeled (about 60)

3 tablespoons cognac

1¼ cups sweet wine, such as Orange Muscat

Kosher salt

Freshly ground black pepper

Fill a very large casserole with 4 quarts of water and bring to a rolling boil over high heat. Carefully lower the lamb into the water and boil for 15 minutes. Drain the lamb and pat dry with paper towels.

Preheat the oven to 200°F.

Heat the oil in the casserole until it sizzles. Add the lamb and cook over moderate heat until nicely browned on all sides. Pour off any fat in the pan. Add the garlic cloves, then add the cognac and carefully light it with a long match or lighter. When the flames die down, add the wine and season the lamb generously with salt and pepper. Cover with a crumpled sheet of wet parchment paper and the lid.

Transfer the casserole to the oven and bake for 6 hours, turning the lamb after 3 hours. Remove from the oven and let stand, uncovered, for 30 minutes.

Transfer the lamb to a platter. Remove the garlic with a slotted spoon and arrange the cloves around the lamb. If there is a lot of liquid left, boil it down until it is thickened and very flavorful. Serve the lamb with the cooking juices. Buttered and rosemary-speckled roasted new potatoes would go very well.

Sometimes Lucky visits Lennie on one of his location shoots. She loves it when he's out in the wild and there is nobody around except the film crew and the actors. One time they were in Arizona, and Lennie took everyone to dinner. It was a blast, especially when the restaurant served the dish they were most famous for—lamb so moist and tender that you can eat it with a spoon.

Lucky loved it so much that she asked for the recipe, and one of these days—when she's not too busy ruling her Vegas empire—she plans to make it.

Lennie teases her that it won't be anytime soon! How well he knows his wife.

Roasted Veal Scallops with Vegetables

Yield: 4 servings

This dish works best when the weather is blustery and guests are feeling slightly fragile. Ask your butcher for a pound of veal bones a day or two in advance of making this delicious entrée.

Divide the garlic into 8 portions and spread each portion over both sides of each veal scallop. Grind the pepper over both sides of each scallop. Place the scallops in a sealable plastic bag and refrigerate for 24 hours.

In a large saucepan, cover the veal bones, carrots, celery, potato, tomato, and onion with water and bring to a boil. Simmer for 2 hours, then strain and discard all the solids. Reduce the stock to a saucelike consistency, and season with salt to taste.

Preheat the oven to 350°F.

Place the eggs in a pie plate and put the bread crumbs on a plate. Dip each scallop in the eggs, then dredge in the crumbs. Place on a rack set on a baking sheet.

Melt the butter in a large skillet over medium-high heat until bubbling and hot. Fry the veal scallops, in batches if necessary, for just over 5 minutes, turning once.

Place the veal scallops in a baking dish and pour over just enough sauce to cover them. Bake the scallops in the oven for 10 minutes. Serve 2 scallops per person, with any remaining sauce heated and poured over the rice.

8 veal scallops, flattened to ¼-inch thickness

3 garlic cloves, finely minced

Freshly ground black pepper

1 pound veal bones

2 carrots, peeled and roughly chopped

2 celery stalks, roughly chopped

1 medium tomato, peeled and sliced

2 large yellow onions, peeled and chopped

Kosher salt

2 large eggs, beaten

1 cup dry bread crumbs

2 tablespoons unsalted butter

Steamed rice, for serving

Shrimp in Lemony Coconut Milk

Yield: 4 to 6 servings

Called moquecca in Brazil, this is a type of seafood stew that can be made with any firm-fleshed fish, and can include shrimp or crab—feel free to use any combination of fish and shellfish. The seafood is poached in a rich, coconut milk broth flavored with butter, lemon juice, and tomatoes. It is usually served with rice. I like the dish served with a mixture of long-grain white rice and black "Forbidden rice."

2 pounds medium shrimp, peeled and deveined, shells reserved

3 cups water

3 tablespoons unsalted butter

1 tablespoon canola oil

1 small onion, diced

2 large tomatoes, roughly chopped, or one 14-ounce can diced organic tomatoes (preferably Muir Glen)

One 14-ounce can unsweetened coconut milk

2 tablespoons freshly squeezed lemon juice

¼ cup cilantro leaves, minced

Tabasco sauce

Salt

Freshly ground black pepper

1 cup cooked long-grain white rice

½ cup cooked black "Forbidden rice," or wild rice

In a medium saucepan, combine the shrimp shells with the water. Boil until the liquid has reduced to ¾ of a cup, about 10 minutes, adding the shrimp meat during the last 2 minutes. Strain and set the stock aside. Pick out and discard the shells and reserve the shrimp meat.

Heat the butter with the canola oil in a large, heavy-bottomed saucepan over medium-high heat. Add the onion and sauté until slightly softened, about 3 minutes. Add the tomatoes and sauté 1 minute. Add the reserved stock, coconut milk, and lemon juice and bring to a boil. Lower the heat, and add the shrimp meat. Turn off the heat, season to taste with the Tabasco, salt, and pepper, ladle over the rice, and serve at once.

"Remember when we took a trip to Brazil," Lucky said to Lennie as they strolled along the Malibu shoreline, the sea lapping at their bare feet.

"Sure. You think I could ever forget?" Lennie responded.

"I loved Rio," Lucky said dreamily. "The people, the beaches, the music, and especially the food."

"Ah yes," Lennie agreed, reaching for his wife's hand.

"Remember that little restaurant where we had that delicious coconut shrimp?" Lucky reminisced.

"I'll never forget it, 'cause if you remember, after we left there you insisted we go to the beach, where you proceeded to take advantage of me."

Lucky laughed. "Great shrimp and sex on the beach. I think you got yourself the perfect wife."

Now it was Lennie's turn to laugh—"And you'll get no argument from me. The shrimp was memorable."

"And the sex?"

"Hey—" Lennie grinned. "Need you ask?"

Santangelo Salmon

Yield: 2 ample servings

Red miso gives the salmon a certain oomph. It is less salty than yellow miso, and goes best with fish. Be sure to use high-quality sake.

Preheat the broiler.

For the salmon: Combine the brown sugar, soy sauce, hot water, and miso and whisk until the sugar has dissolved. Set aside.

Choose a gratin dish large enough to hold the salmon without crowding, and lightly coat it with oil. Arrange the salmon fillets in the dish, and spread the miso mixture evenly over each fillet. Broil the fillets, basting with the miso mixture once or twice, for 7 to 8 minutes for medium rare, or 10 minutes for medium, or until the fillets flake easily when prodded with a fork.

For the sake butter: Meanwhile, in a small saucepan over medium heat, soften the ginger and shallots in the butter for 3 to 4 minutes. Pour in ½ cup of the sake, bring the mixture to a boil, and reduce to about 3 tablespoons, about 3 minutes. Pour in the half-and-half, return to a boil, and reduce by about half, about 2 minutes. Increase the heat to medium-high, and, whisking constantly, add the butter, one cube at a time. The butter should create a thick and creamy sauce. When all of the butter has been incorporated, remove the saucepan from the heat and whisk in the remaining 1 teaspoon of sake and the lime juice. Season to taste with salt and white pepper. Using an immersion blender or in a stand blender purée the sauce, in batches, until very smooth.

Divide the sake butter between two plates, top with the basmati rice and then the salmon, and serve at once.

SALMON
⅓ cup packed dark brown sugar

3 tablespoons low-sodium soy sauce

2 tablespoons hot water

2 tablespoons red miso

Canola oil, for coating the dish

Four 1-inch thick salmon fillets, pinbones removed

1 tablespoon minced chives

SAKE BUTTER
2 tablespoons peeled and minced fresh ginger

1 tablespoon finely chopped shallots

1 tablespoon unsalted butter

½ cup good-quality sake, plus 1 teaspoon

2 tablespoons half-and-half

8 tablespoons (½ stick) cold, unsalted butter, cut into ¼-inch cubes

Juice of 1 lime wedge

Kosher salt

Freshly ground white pepper

Cooked basmati rice

Skate with Lobster Rice

Yield: 2 servings

3 cups lobster stock (Better than Bouillon Lobster Base makes a fine quick substitute)

½ cup dry white vermouth

2 tablespoons unsalted butter

One 14-ounce can light, unsweetened coconut milk, shaken well

½ teaspoon cayenne pepper (no more!)

1 teaspoon ground ginger

4 saffron strands

2 teaspoons minced lemongrass

2 teaspoons shredded, unsweetened coconut, lightly toasted

curry leaves (optional)

1½ cups long-grain rice

1 cup frozen peas

1 tablespoon cornstarch, dissolved in 1 tablespoon water, if needed to thicken

Two 10-ounce boneless, skinless skate wings (see headnote)

Sea salt

Freshly ground white pepper

2 to 3 tablespoons minced scallions (optional)

This lobster rice is also excellent with hanger steak, cooked separately, instead of skate—a kind of surf-and-turf.

In a deep skillet large enough to hold both skate wings in a single layer, bring the lobster stock, vermouth, butter, coconut milk, cayenne, ginger, saffron, lemongrass, toasted coconut, and optional curry leaves to a boil. Stir in the rice. Reduce to a simmer, cover, and cook for 20 minutes. Stir in the peas and, if the mixture seems too runny to you, add the cornstarch slurry and stir until the mixture thickens, 1 to 2 minutes.

Season the skate wings with sea salt and white pepper, lower the fish into the stock, and poach, covered, at a bare simmer until a knife slides easily into natural divisions in the fish, 3 to 4 minutes. Spoon the lobster rice into large, low bowls and lay the skate wings over the rice. Scatter generously with the scallions, if using.

Sole with Parmesan Crust

Yield: 2 servings

A surprising and delectable seafood entrée, this sole dish—which can work with other finfish fillets—is also quick and easy. But an important key to this dish is not to overcook the fish. Just barely heat the fish through on the stovetop so that when the broiler is used to crisp the crust, the fish doesn't overcook in the extreme heat. The crust can also be used to coat other fish, such as salmon or halibut.

Preheat the broiler. In a small bowl, stir together the butter, panko, cheese, onion, and rosemary until blended. Season with salt and pepper and set aside.

Heat the oil in a large sauté pan over medium-high heat. Season the fillets with salt and pepper. When the oil is hot, but not smoking, add the fillets to the pan and cook, turning once, just until opaque in the center, 2 to 3 minutes per side. Transfer the fish to a baking pan or lined baking sheet.

Using your hands, spread the seasoned crumbs over the top of each fish to a thickness of ¼ inch. Set the pan under the broiler about 4 inches from the heat and broil watchfully just until the crust is golden brown, 2 to 3 minutes.

Remove the pan from the oven and serve the fish at once.

4 tablespoons (½ stick) unsalted butter, at room temperature

½ cup panko (Japanese-style bread crumbs)

¼ cup grated Parmigiano-Reggiano cheese

1 small onion or medium shallot, finely chopped

1 teaspoon finely chopped fresh rosemary

Sea salt

Freshly ground black pepper

1 tablespoon olive oil

2 skinless striped bass fillets (6 to 8 ounces each)

Delicious Side Dishes

New Potato Salad

Potato Balls Sautéed in Butter

The Best Mashed Potatoes Ever!

English Roast Potatoes

Roasted Butternut Squash

Sweet Potatoes and Apricots

Creamy Peas with Tarragon

Green Beans with Cumin for a Crowd

Slow-Braised Green Beans

Creamed Fresh Corn–Stuffed Red Bell Peppers

Roasted Broccoli with Fondue

Brussels Sprouts Moutarde

Cheesy Cauliflower Gratin

Blue Cheese and Caramelized Onion Potatoes au Gratin

Crabby Portobello Mushrooms

New Potato Salad

Yield: enough for 4 servings

1½ to 2 pounds tiny new potatoes, a little bigger than marbles, halved or quartered if not, washed and patted dry

2 tablespoons extra-virgin olive oil, or duck or bacon fat

Kosher salt

Freshly ground black pepper

2 tablespoons tarragon-infused white vinegar

1 celery stalk, diced

3 to 4 scallions, white and light green parts only (or shallots), minced

½ pound ham, sliced into bite-size pieces or strips (or good-quality bacon, fried and diced)

1 tablespoon minced fresh chives

½ cup crème fraîche

2 tablespoons mayonnaise

2 to 3 tablespoons chopped fresh tarragon leaves, or 1 tablespoon dried

1 tablespoon minced fresh thyme (or 1 teaspoon dried)

Slices of hard-cooked egg

½ pound smoked trout, skin and bones discarded, flaked

Make this recipe when you have some leftover roasted ham on hand. The first steps of this recipe may be used to provide great roasted potatoes for a side dish. And if new potatoes are at hand, so are fresh herbs: please try to use them. You'll probably want to double this, if you're going to the trouble. But don't crowd the potatoes in the roasting skillet, or they'll steam and never achieve that roasted flavor. And be sure to serve the salad at room temperature or slightly warmer.

Preheat the oven to 400°F. Preheat a large, cast-iron skillet over high heat for several minutes. Add the olive oil, and carefully stir in the potatoes. (A splatter screen would be quite useful here.) Sauté the potatoes for 5 minutes, shaking the skillet often after the first 2 minutes. Season with salt and pepper to taste.

Transfer the skillet to the oven. Roast the potatoes for 20 minutes, or until tender, giving the skillet a couple of shakes after 10 minutes to redistribute the potatoes.

Transfer the potatoes to a large bowl. Stir in the tarragon vinegar. Bring to room temperature. Stir in the remaining ingredients. Taste carefully, you might want more crème fraîche or salt. Serve at once, with an extravagant dollop of crème fraîche and the chopped chives on top. Come to think of it, a decorative tablespoon of good salmon roe would be most welcome, too. Finish with slices of hard-cooked egg, if desired, and/or scattered with the optional smoked trout flakes.

Potato Balls Sautéed in Butter

Yield: 8 to 10 servings

I guarantee you won't have any leftovers from this dish. This relatively simple recipe needs only two ingredients: butter and russet potatoes. Every time I've made these, everyone wanted more, including me!

Peel the potatoes and place them in a bowl of cold water. Using a 1¼-inch melon baller, scoop as many balls from the potatoes as possible, and transfer them to another bowl of cold water as cut.

5 pounds russet potatoes

8 tablespoons (1 stick) unsalted butter

Kosher salt

Drain the potato balls, then parboil them in boiling salted water for 5 minutes. Drain in a colander and let them air-dry for 2 minutes.

Heat the butter in a 12-inch, nonstick skillet over moderately high heat until the foam subsides. Add the potatoes and sauté, shaking the skillet frequently, until golden, 10 to 12 minutes. Season with salt and, using a slotted spoon, transfer the potatoes to a serving bowl.

The Best Mashed Potatoes Ever!

Yield: about 10 servings

Everyone loves mashed potatoes, and these are just the best.

6 large Yukon gold potatoes (about 3 pounds)

2 teaspoons salt

Freshly ground black pepper

12 tablespoons (1½ sticks) unsalted butter, softened

⅔ cup heavy cream

Peel the potatoes and cut them into 1-inch wedges. Put them in a large saucepan and cover with cold water. Bring to a boil, reduce the heat to simmer, and cook until tender, 20 to 30 minutes.

Drain the potatoes and pass them through a ricer back into the large bowl. Season with the salt and pepper and stir in the softened butter and cream, adding more or less cream according to your desired consistency. Keep on whipping! It's well worth it.

Lucky survived many childhood tragedies and went on to prosper and become the dynamic, fierce, and wildly popular woman she is today.

Memories of her mother are bittersweet, but she will never forget the hugs and cuddles, and the feel of her mom's smooth skin. And sometimes, when it was just the two of them at home alone, she would help her mom make The Best Mashed Potatoes Ever!

Fond and special memories. Comfort food. Lucky never forgets those special moments.

English Roast Potatoes

Yield: 6 servings

So crisp on the outside and deliciously soft on the inside.

Peel the potatoes and cut them into 3-inch wedges. Parboil them for 10 minutes, or until they are only slightly cooked.

Coat a roasting pan with olive oil, and preheat in the oven to 400°F for 5 minutes. When the oil is hot, put potatoes in the preheated pan, cover with a sprinkling of salt, pepper, mixed herbs, and paprika, and the butter.

Bake the potatoes for 20 minutes, reduce the oven temperature to 350°F, and continue to bake for 30 minutes more. The potatoes should be crisp and brown, and ready to enjoy!

8 large russet potatoes

extra-virgin olive oil

Freshly ground black pepper

A scattering of salt (Kosher salt or coarse sea salt)

A scattering of chopped fresh herbs

Sweet paprika

4 tablespoons (½ stick) unsalted butter, cut into ½-inch pieces

English Roast Potatoes are a teenage Gino junior's passion. He devours them. And Lucky knows if Gino junior is home for dinner she'd better make double the amount. Ah . . . teenage boys . . . they never stop eating—especially when roast potatoes are on the menu.

Roasted Butternut Squash

Yield: 2 to 4 servings, depending on the size of the squash

With such a delicately flavored earthy squash, less is more.

1 medium butternut squash

Unsalted butter

Freshly ground black pepper

Kosher salt

Preheat the oven to 400°F. Carefully split the squash, scrape out the seeds and strings, and roast, split sides down, in a roasting pan with ¼ inch of water in it, until tender, 45 to 90 minutes, depending on the size of the squash.

Serve with plenty of unsalted butter and a good grinding of black pepper, and season with salt to taste.

Lucky and Venus often enjoy a quick lunch if they can fit it into their busy schedules. Sometimes Lucky races her Ferrari over to Venus's house, and they sit out on the terrace and enjoy a quick meal of roasted butternut squash. So good, and yet quick and easy to prepare.

Lucky enjoys giving Venus advice about her love life. Venus never listens—she's having too much fun with random boy toys!

"One of these days you'll find a man like Lennie," Lucky informs her.

"Unfortunately there is only one Lennie," Venus replies. "So maybe one of these days I'll be forced to steal him from you."

Lucky laughs in her face. Lennie is hers, and beware the woman who ever attempts to lure him away.

Sweet Potatoes and Apricots

Yield: about 8 servings

The bourbon that plumps the dried apricots also really hoists the flavor of this Southern classic.

Warm the bourbon in the microwave until just under boiling. Place the chopped dried apricots in a medium bowl and pour the hot bourbon over them. Set aside for 20 to 30 minutes, stirring a few times.

Preheat the oven to 350°F.

Scrub the sweet potatoes and pierce them several times with a fine skewer or a fork. Arrange the potatoes on a baking sheet in a single layer. Bake the potatoes until they're quite soft, 60 to 90 minutes. Remove from the oven, leaving the oven on, and let the potatoes stand until they cool, about 20 minutes.

Peel the potatoes with a knife or peeler and put them in a large bowl. Add the brown sugar, butter, and vanilla and mash with a fork or potato masher until blended, stopping when the potatoes are still slightly chunky. Stir in the bourbon and chopped apricots. Transfer the mixture to a roomy baking dish.

Bake, uncovered, in the oven until the mixture is heated through, 20 to 30 minutes. Serve hot or warm.

¼ cup good bourbon

⅓ cup chopped dried apricots

4 pounds sweet potatoes

¼ cup packed dark brown sugar

4 tablespoons (½ stick) unsalted butter, softened

1 teaspoon vanilla extract

Creamy Peas with Tarragon

Yield: 4 servings

Don't thaw the peas before adding them to the skillet.

2 tablespoons unsalted butter

1 shallot, minced

1 tablespoon minced fresh tarragon

1 garlic clove, minced

½ cup heavy cream

1 pound frozen peas (about 3 cups)

2 teaspoons sugar

Kosher salt

Freshly ground black pepper

Melt the butter in a 12-inch, nonstick skillet over medium-high heat. Add the minced shallot, tarragon, and garlic and cook until softened, about 2 minutes. Stir in the heavy cream and simmer until thickened, about 2 minutes. Stir in the peas and the sugar. Cover and cook just until the peas are thawed and heated through, about 4 minutes. Season with salt and pepper to taste.

Green Beans with Cumin for a Crowd

Yield: 10 servings

Giving green beans a Middle Eastern accent widens their appeal considerably. Use black cumin seeds if you can find them. They have a more complex, peppery flavor than the much more common amber cumin seeds. If your "crowd" likes spicy food, by all means increase the amount of cayenne pepper.

Bring a large saucepan of water to a boil. Add the beans, return the water to a boil, and cook for 2 minutes. Drain the beans and cool them under cold running water in a colander.

Combine the oil and cumin in a large wok or frying pan over medium heat. Cook, stirring, 1 minute. Add the ginger and cook, stirring, 1 minute.

Add the beans and stir to coat with the oil and spices. Sprinkle with the salt and stir. Cover, turn the heat down to very low, and cook, stirring 3 to 4 times, until the beans are tender and lightly browned, 10 to 15 minutes.

Stir in the lime juice and sprinkle with the cayenne. Stir well and salt to taste. Serve hot.

2½ pounds green beans, both ends trimmed

⅓ cup canola oil

3 teaspoons cumin seeds

One 3-inch piece fresh ginger, peeled and finely grated

1½ teaspoons kosher salt

3 tablespoons freshly squeezed lime juice

½ teaspoon cayenne pepper

Slow-Braised Green Beans

Yield: 4 to 6 servings

"Crisp-tender" green beans are considered by many cooks (including myself) to be under-cooked. This recipe is a reminder of how they were cooked when I was a child.

It takes very little effort to achieve this magical texture: all you have to do is throw all your ingredients into a pot, cover it, put it over reasonably low heat, and wait for two hours. The hardest part, in fact, is trimming the beans before you cook them. You'll need to cut or snap off the stem end (the blunt rather than pointy end), which takes a while when you're dealing with two pounds of beans. But once you've tasted the finished product, you'll do it again and again. I usually skip the dill and yogurt, but it's worth a try to include them.

2 pounds green beans

1 large red onion, chopped

1 large tomato, chopped

⅓ cup extra-virgin olive oil

Juice of 1 lemon

2 garlic cloves, pressed

⅔ cup water

Kosher salt

Freshly ground black pepper

¼ cup chopped fresh dill (optional)

½ cup Greek yogurt (optional)

Put the green beans, onion, tomato, olive oil, lemon juice, and garlic in a medium pot. Add the water and season with salt and pepper. Cover and cook over medium-low heat until the green beans are so tender that they're falling apart, about 2 hours.

Stir in most of the dill if using. Taste and adjust the seasoning. Serve hot or at room temperature, garnished with the remaining dill and the yogurt if desired. (Store leftover green beans in an airtight container in the refrigerator for up to a few days.)

Creamed Fresh Corn-Stuffed Red Bell Peppers

Yield: 4 servings, very good reheated

These make a terrific late-summer entrée, when peppers and corn peak in flavor.

Corn kernels are best removed with a sharp knife: Hold the cob straight up in a bowl that fits into your sink, and cut with an even, downward sawing motion. Then scrape the cob back and forth with the back of the knife to get out the pulp and milk.

If this is to be an entrée, serve it with a side of garlic bread and caprese: a row of tomato and buffalo mozzarella slices garnished with basil and drizzled with superb extra-virgin olive oil.

Prep all of the ingredients before commencing.

In a medium saucepan, cook the diced bacon until just crisp over medium heat. Using a slotted spoon, transfer the bacon to the corn bowl and pour out all but 2 tablespoons of the drippings. Through the large holes of a box grater, grate in most of the onion and cook over medium heat, stirring every so often, for 3 to 4 minutes. Deglaze the pan with the Calvados. Stir in the corn kernels and bacon, chopped olives, roasted bell pepper, and bacon. Add a pinch of salt and a few grinds of black pepper, and cook for 4 minutes, stirring often. Then keep mixture just at the simmer.

Slice the tops off the raw bell peppers, scoop out the seeds, and trim off any membranes from the inner walls. Rinse and place them in an 8-inch Pyrex glass baking dish or pie plate. Seal tightly with plastic wrap, and microwave on high for 3 to 5 minutes, or until fairly tender, but not mushy. (Microwave ovens vary widely in power from 750 to 1200 watts; consult the manual that accompanied your oven for timing recommendations.) Remove the plastic wrap, drain any collected fluid from inside and around the peppers, and keep them warm.

¼ pound slab bacon, or pancetta sliced into ¼-inch dice (frozen briefly for easier slicing)

1 medium-large yellow onion, peeled

3 large ears of fresh corn, kernels removed

10 to 12 pimiento-stuffed green olives, thinly sliced crosswise

1 large red bell pepper, roasted or broiled, chopped, and tossed with the corn

4 meaty red bell peppers, shaped to stand comfortably

1 tablespoon Calvados

2 large egg yolks

½ cup heavy cream

(continued)

Freshly grated nutmeg (about ½ teaspoon)

1½ cups grated truffled sheep's milk cheese, or soft goat cheese, such as chèvre

Meanwhile, in a small bowl, beat the egg yolks with a fork until light yellow, then blend in the cream. Pour into the hot corn-bacon mixture, and stir over low heat for a few minutes to thicken. Stir in the nutmeg.

Fill the peppers with the hot mixture, divide the grated cheese over the top of each filled pepper, and run the peppers under the broiler until the cheese bubbles and the tops of the peppers are starting to blacken. Serve at once.

Variations

- Add ½ cup cooked rice to the filling. Try wild rice.

- Instead of microwaving the peppers, braise them in chicken broth just until tender, 5 to 6 minutes.

- Stuff poblano peppers instead of bell peppers. Use 8 of the largest poblanos you can find, estimating 2 peppers per serving. Since poblanos won't "stand," oil them lightly and broil them whole (stem intact) or roast them on the stovetop over an open flame until their skins blacken. As soon as they're cool enough to handle, rub off most of the blackened skins with paper towels. Slit the peppers and remove the seeds and ribs. Fill the peppers and line them up in a gratin dish. Sprinkle the cheeses over the peppers and broil until the cheese melts completely. Serve topped with a dollop of crème fraîche and a scattering of minced chives.

Roasted Broccoli with Fondue

Yield: 2 to 4 servings

Even those who claim to dislike broccoli will lunge for this dish.

One 1½-pound head broccoli, cut into long spears

Two 1½-inch-thick slices peasant bread, crusts removed, cut into 1½-inch cubes

¼ cup, plus 2 tablespoons olive oil

1 large garlic clove, pressed

Kosher salt

Freshly ground black pepper

¼ cup plus 2 tablespoons heavy cream

1 large egg yolk

2 ounces fontina cheese, shredded

1 tablespoon very finely chopped fresh marjoram

1½ teaspoons balsamic vinegar

Preheat the oven to 450°F. Heat a large rimmed baking sheet in the oven until it is very hot. In a large bowl, press the garlic clove into the olive oil and season the oil generously with salt and pepper. Toss the broccoli spears with the bread cubes in the olive oil. Spread the broccoli and bread cubes on the hot baking sheet and roast for 15 to 20 minutes, turning once, until the broccoli is tender and browned in spots and the bread cubes are crisp and golden.

Meanwhile, in a small saucepan, heat the cream until boiling. In a small bowl, whisk the egg yolk. Very gradually whisk in the hot cream. Return the mixture to the saucepan and cook over low heat, whisking constantly, until slightly thickened, about 2 minutes. Remove from the heat, add the fontina, and whisk until the cheese has melted. Pour the fondue into a bowl. Transfer the broccoli and bread to plates and sprinkle with the marjoram and balsamic. Serve with the fondue.

Brussels Sprouts Moutarde

Yield: 4 to 6 servings

This dish is a lifesaver at holiday meals, such as Thanksgiving, when the oven and stovetop are already busy, because it can be prepared entirely in a microwave oven. If you need to double this, there will be time to microwave it in two batches, especially if you are serving buffet-style.

Place the bacon strips on paper towels on a large plate, cover with more paper towels, and microwave on full power until medium-crisp, 3 to 4 minutes, depending on your oven's wattage. Roughly chop the bacon.

Place the butter in a large microwave-proof casserole and cover with a loose-fitting lid. Microwave on full power for 1 minute, or until the butter has melted. Stir in everything else, adding the bacon and sprouts last. Mix well.

Microwave on full power for 4 to 9 minutes, depending on your oven's wattage and your preference for al dente Brussels sprouts. (Start testing and stirring at 4 minutes.)

5 strips thickly sliced bacon

5 tablespoons (½ stick plus 1 tablespoon) unsalted butter

3 tablespoons smooth Dijon mustard, such as Maille

2 teaspoons dried tarragon (or thyme, if you don't like tarragon)

2 teaspoons freshly squeezed lemon juice

1 teaspoon finely grated lemon zest

½ teaspoon vanilla extract

½ cup low-sodium chicken broth

1 teaspoon balsamic vinegar

3 good splashes of dry white vermouth

2 pounds Brussels sprouts, rinsed, trimmed, and halved lengthwise

Cheesy Cauliflower Gratin

Yield: 4 servings

It's no secret that cheese can seduce even a fussy child into eating vegetables.

Preheat the oven to 375°F. Boil the cauliflower florets in a large pot of boiling salted water for 5 to 6 minutes. Drain and set aside.

Melt 2 tablespoons of the butter in a medium saucepan over low heat. Add the flour, stirring constantly with a wooden spoon for 2 minutes. Pour the hot milk into the butter-flour mixture and stir until it comes to a boil. Boil, whisking constantly, for 1 minute, or until thickened. Remove from the heat, add 1 teaspoon of salt, the pepper, nutmeg, ½ cup of the Gruyère, the cheddar, and the Parmigiano-Reggiano.

Pour one-third of the sauce over the bottom of a large gratin dish. Place the drained cauliflower over the sauce and then spread the rest of the sauce evenly over the top. Combine the bread crumbs with the remaining cheese and sprinkle on top. Melt the remaining 2 tablespoons butter and drizzle over the gratin. Sprinkle with salt and pepper. Bake for 25 to 30 minutes until the top has browned. Serve hot or at room temperature.

1 head cauliflower, cut into large florets

4 tablespoons (½ stick) unsalted butter

3 tablespoons all-purpose flour

2 cups hot whole milk

1 teaspoon kosher salt

½ teaspoon freshly ground black pepper

¼ teaspoon freshly grated nutmeg

¾ cup freshly grated Gruyère cheese

½ cup shredded cheddar cheese

½ cup freshly grated Parmigiano-Reggiano cheese

¼ cup seasoned dried bread crumbs

Blue Cheese and Caramelized Onion Potatoes au Gratin

Yield: at least 8 servings

CARAMELIZED ONIONS
Olive oil

Unsalted butter

2 small (or 1 large) onions, thinly sliced

Kosher salt

Pinch of sugar

GRATIN
4 cups red potatoes, peeled and cut into ⅛-inch-thick slices

¾ cup crumbled blue cheese

½ cup grated Gruyère cheese

2 garlic cloves

1 sprig fresh thyme

2 cups heavy cream

½ teaspoon kosher salt plus more as needed

Freshly ground black pepper

For the caramelized onions: In a large, heavy-bottomed pan heat about 1 tablespoon each of butter and oil. Add the onions, sprinkle with salt, toss to coat, and spread evenly. Turn the heat to medium-low and let the onions slowly caramelize, at least 45 minutes. Stir occasionally to prevent the onions from browning too quickly; you may have to adjust heat. If onions are browning too quickly, add a splash of water to the pan and stir.

After about 15 minutes add sugar, and a little more oil if the onions start sticking to the pan. Continue to stir the onions and scrape up the brown bits on the bottom of the pan until the onions develop a nice, deep brown color. Preheat oven to 400°F.

For the gratin: Ready the potatoes and place them in a large bowl of cold water while you prepare the other ingredients. When complete, drain the potatoes.

In a medium to large pot, combine the potatoes, cream, garlic, thyme, salt, and pepper and bring to a boil, stirring often. As soon as the potatoes come to a boil, reduce the heat to a simmer. Continue to cook for a few minutes, stirring, until the cream thickens slightly. Remove the pot from the heat. Remove the thyme stem.

Butter all sides of your cast-iron skillets or baking dish and add one-third of the potatoes to the bottom. Top with one-third of the onion and one-third of the blue cheese. Sprinkle a layer of kosher salt and pepper on top of each layer as you go. Repeat the layering two more times with the blue cheese layer on top. Sprinkle the Gruyère on top of the final blue cheese layer. Pour all of the cream on top of the potatoes. Cover with aluminum foil and place the skillets or baking dish on a large baking sheet in case the potatoes bubble over.

Bake for 30 minutes. Uncover, and bake for another 10 minutes, or until the cheese bubbles and browns and the potatoes are knife-tender.

Crabby Portobello Mushrooms

Yield: 6 servings

These make such a winning side dish, more than a few of my dinner guests have ignored their entrées and devoured this instead.

Position a rack in the top third of the oven and preheat the oven to 400°F. Lightly oil a baking sheet, or line the sheet with parchment paper.

For the crabmeat: Mix together the crab, egg, panko, mayonnaise, scallions, Worcestershire sauce, Old Bay Seasoning, salt, and Tabasco until combined.

For the mushrooms: Trim the mushroom stems flush with the caps and discard the stems. Rinse the mushrooms quickly under cold running water and wipe them dry with paper towels, to remove any grit. Using the tip of a spoon, scrape out the dark gills from the undersides of the caps. Fill each mushroom cap with the crab mixture, mounding the filling in the cap. Place the caps, filling sides up, on the baking sheet. Sprinkle the filling in each cap with 1 tablespoon of panko and drizzle with the oil.

Bake until the panko is golden brown, 20 to 25 minutes. Serve hot with the lemon wedges on the side. If you're being fancy, wrap the lemon wedges in a layer of cheesecloth to keep any seeds at bay.

CRABMEAT FILLING

1 pound crabmeat, picked over for shell bits

1 large egg, beaten

½ cup panko (Japanese-style bread crumbs)

¼ cup mayonnaise

¼ cup finely chopped scallions

1 teaspoon Worcestershire sauce

1 teaspoon Old Bay Seasoning

¼ teaspoon salt

¼ teaspoon Tabasco sauce

6 portobello mushrooms, about 3½ inches in diameter

6 tablespoons panko, for topping

Olive oil, for drizzling

Lemon wedges, for serving

Incredible Sauces

Cranberry-Orange Chutney

Plum Glaze

Barbecue "Gonzalez" Sauce

Lucky's Best Besciamella Sauce

Blender Hollandaise Sauce

Cranberry-Orange Chutney

Yield: about 2 cups chutney

Cranberries can vary considerably in sourness, so taste the sauce while adding the sugar.

12 ounces cranberries, about 3 cups, at room temperature (Ocean Spray packages cranberries in 12-ounce increments)

¾ cup Port wine

¼ cup balsamic vinegar

⅓ cup sugar, or to taste (see headnote)

2 pinches of kosher salt

Juice and finely grated zest of 1 orange

1 teaspoon cornstarch

½ teaspoon dry mustard, or to taste

1 teaspoon freshly squeezed lemon juice

1 teaspoon finely grated lemon zest

A pinch of ground cloves, allspice, and ginger, or pumpkin pie seasoning

¼ cup golden raisins, reconstituted in hot water or hot red wine (optional)

Combine the berries, Port, and balsamic in a large, heavy-bottomed, saucepan over medium-high heat. Cook until most of the berries burst, stirring occasionally, about 10 minutes. Add the sugar and salt, and stir for 1 minute.

Meanwhile, combine the orange juice and orange zest, cornstarch, mustard, lemon juice, and lemon zest, and spices in a medium bowl and whisk until smooth. Stir the orange mixture into the hot berry mixture. Stir in the raisins if using. Simmer until thickened, about 5 minutes.

Taste carefully. Need more sugar? I doubt it!

Plum Glaze

Yield: about 1 cup glaze

Combine all of the ingredients in a food processor and pulse until smooth.

About an hour before you're finished roasting a duck, chicken, or pork loin, paint the glaze all over the bird or pork. Glaze again every 15 minutes until done.

½ cup smooth plum jelly

2 tablespoons orange marmalade

Juice of 1 orange, freshly squeezed

2 teaspoons garlic powder

1 teaspoon onion powder

2 teaspoons ground ginger

1 tablespoon low-sodium soy sauce

1 tablespoon freshly ground white pepper

Barbecue "Gonzalez" Sauce

Yield: 1½ cups sauce

Combine all of the ingredients in a small saucepan and simmer over low heat for 10 minutes. Remove from heat and let cool.

The sauce will keep for 10 days, refrigerated.

1 cup ketchup

2 shallots, minced

1 garlic clove, pressed

¼ cup Worcestershire sauce

Juice of 1 lemon

2 teaspoons molasses

2 teaspoons malt vinegar

1 teaspoon kosher salt

1 teaspoon dry mustard

2 jalapeño peppers, stemmed, seeded, and minced

1 habanero pepper, stemmed, seeded, and minced (optional)

1 teaspoon crushed red pepper flakes

½ teaspoon Tabasco sauce

2 pinches of dried thyme

Lucky's Best Besciamella Sauce

Yield: about 1 cup sauce

2 tablespoons unsalted butter

2 tablespoons instant flour, such as Wondra

1¼ cups whole milk

Kosher salt

Freshly ground white pepper

Over medium-high heat, melt the butter in a medium, heavy-bottomed saucepan. Add the flour and cook, stirring constantly, until the mixture bubbles lightly, 2 to 3 minutes. Don't let the mixture brown.

Meanwhile, heat the milk in a glass measure in the microwave until nearly boiling. When the flour mixture is ready, slowly add the hot milk, stirring until the sauce thickens. Now bring it to a boil. Taste carefully, and season with salt and white pepper to taste. Lower the heat and cook, still stirring, for 2 to 3 minutes longer. Remove from heat.

If you're not using the sauce right away, press a layer of waxed paper directly onto the surface to prevent a film from forming.

Blender Hollandaise Sauce

Yield: 5 to 6 servings

This is every bit as good as the endlessly stirred double-boiler hollandaise—but so much quicker and easier. The tarragon tilts the hollandaise toward béarnaise sauce.

Start this sauce only a few minutes before serving.

Combine the egg yolks, mustard, lemon juice, tarragon, and Tabasco sauce in the jar of a blender. Cover and blend for 10 seconds. Let the mixture rest while you melt the butter in a glass measure in the microwave oven. When the butter is hot, but not browned, turn the blender on high and pour the hot butter into the egg mixture in a steady stream. The mixture will thicken instantly. Pour the sauce over or around whatever you are serving.

3 very fresh large egg yolks

¼ teaspoon smooth Dijon mustard

1 tablespoon freshly squeezed lemon juice (possibly a bit more)

1 teaspoon dried tarragon

1 dash of Tabasco sauce

8 tablespoons (1 stick) unsalted butter

Delectable Desserts

Baked Peaches with Cointreau

Pear Tart

Apple Crumble

Pear and Blueberry Pie with Buttery Oatmeal Crust

Perfect Cherry Pie

Butterscotch Pie

Moist Sugar Cake

Rich Carrot Cake

To-Die-For Cheesecake

Crème Brûlée

Flourless Chocolate Cake

Molten Chocolate Tarts

Intense Lemon Sorbet

Crème Fraîche with Chocolate Mousse

Buttermilk Panna Cotta with Strawberries

Coconut Sorbet

Baked Peaches with Cointreau

This simple but luscious dessert makes for a splendid finish to a high September supper. Be sure to use the best vanilla ice cream you can find—homemade would be heavenly.

Preheat the oven to 300°F. Using a swivel vegetable peeler, peel some freestone white peaches—1 to 2 peaches per person—and leave them whole.

Warm the peaches in the oven during dinner for about 30 minutes.

Serve the peaches over good vanilla ice cream, and drizzle with Cointreau, ¼ to ½ cup per serving, or pass a small pitcher of Cointreau at the table.

Peaches (freestone white if available)

Vanilla ice cream

Cointreau

"I'm making you dessert," Lucky said.

"What have I done to deserve it?" Lennie said, lounging in front of a ball game on TV.

Lucky gave a secretive smile. "It's not what you've done," she said succinctly. "It's all about what you're going to do."

Lennie got her drift and lazily smiled. "You'd better be making that peach thing you do."

"Ah . . . maybe."

"Maybe, huh?"

"Yeah . . . maybe something to shift you off the couch."

"As if I need shifting."

Lucky smiled again. "We'll see," she said, and headed for the kitchen.

Baked peaches steeped in Cointreau. Lennie was going to be one very grateful husband indeed.

Pear Tart

Yield: 4 to 6 servings

This is actually a dense, buttery cake, weighted by the pear juice. Just be careful not to over-cook the tart. Like many dishes, this is even better the next day!

Canola oil, for greasing the pan

8 tablespoons (1 stick) unsalted butter, softened

¾ cup sugar

2 teaspoons vanilla extract

2 large eggs

1 cup all-purpose flour

1 teaspoon baking powder

½ teaspoon salt

2 or 3 ripe juicy pears, peeled, cored, and cut into eighths

Preheat the oven to 350°F.

Pour a little canola oil on a folded paper towel, and rub an 8-inch springform pan lightly with the oil.

In a bowl, cream the butter, sugar, and vanilla with a hand mixer. Add the eggs, one at a time, and beat to incorporate.

Combine the flour, baking powder, and salt, and add to the butter mixture. Do not overbeat the mixture.

Spread the batter in the prepared pan. Press the pear slices into the batter in a pinwheel pattern. Cram in as many as you can. The batter will rise and cover the pears, so they don't have to look perfect. The more pears, the moister the tart will be.

Bake just until a skewer comes out clean, 45 to 55 minutes. If you have any doubts, underbake. You don't want the tart to dry out, and it will continue to cook after it's removed from the oven. Start testing with the skewer at 45 minutes. As it cools, the tart will pull away from the sides of the pan nicely.

Apple Crumble

Yield: 4 to 6 servings

A homey, comforting classic if ever there was one.

Preheat the oven to 375°F. In a large bowl, toss the apple slices with the white and brown sugars and the spices. Let the apples sit for 30 minutes, or until the apples release some of their juice and the sugars are moist.

For the crumble topping: Meanwhile, in another large bowl, combine the flour, oatmeal, and both sugars and mix well with your cool fingertips, breaking up any lumps. Add the butter and work the mixture gently until it resembles coarse crumbs. Cover tightly with plastic wrap and refrigerate until ready to use.

Transfer the apples with their juices to a 1½-quart gratin dish. Pour the melted butter over the apples. Sprinkle the topping evenly over them.

Bake for 30 to 40 minutes until the topping is golden brown and the filling is bubbling. Serve warm, with ice cream, crème fraîche, or whipped cream.

5 to 6 crisp, tart apples such as Granny Smith (about 2 pounds) peeled, cored, and sliced into 1-inch pieces

1 tablespoon sugar

2 tablespoons dark brown sugar

1½ teaspoons ground cinnamon

6 fresh gratings of nutmeg

2 tablespoons unsalted butter, melted

CRUMBLE TOPPING

¾ cup plus 2 tablespoons all-purpose flour

¼ cup plus 2 tablespoons old-fashioned oatmeal

¼ cup granulated sugar

¼ cup plus 3 tablespoons packed dark brown sugar

12 tablespoons (1½ sticks) unsalted butter, cut into ½-inch pieces and slightly softened

Pear and Blueberry Pie with Buttery Oatmeal Crust

Yield: one 10- to 12-inch pie

PIE CRUST

Softened unsalted butter, for greasing the pie pan

2 cups rolled oats, or old-fashioned oatmeal

1 cup all-purpose flour

¾ cup packed dark brown sugar

½ teaspoon sea salt

1 teaspoon ground cinnamon

6 fresh gratings of nutmeg

1 teaspoon vanilla extract

12 tablespoons (1½ sticks) unsalted butter, melted

FILLING

4 cups blueberries, picked over, washed at the last minute, and dried gently with paper towels

1 heaping tablespoon orange zest, or more, finely minced, if you like

1 teaspoon lemon zest, finely grated (optional)

2 tablespoons all-purpose flour

The filling for this hearty dessert tastes especially fresh because it gets only 25 minutes in the oven and it's considerably refreshed by the presence of a whole tablespoon of orange—and, if you want, a bit of lemon—zest. I don't add sugar to the filling, because I don't like fruit to be cloyingly sweet, but by all means suit yourself. The first piece cut from the pie will usually be a delicious mess.

Preheat the oven to 325°F. Butter a 10-inch glass pie pan (for a thick oatmeal crust; a 12 inch for a thin crust).

For the crust: In a food processor fitted with the steel blade, process the oats, flour, sugar, salt, cinnamon, nutmeg, and vanilla to blend. Add the melted butter and process just until combined. The dough will be stiff. Press the dough into and up the sides of the prepared pan. Bake for 15 minutes.

For the filling: In a low, wide bowl, gently combine all of the filling ingredients. Pour into the prebaked crust and return to the oven for 25 minutes, or just until crust begins to brown lightly. Transfer to a wire rack to cool.

Serve warm or at room temperature with a good dollop of crème fraîche or vanilla ice cream.

Perfect Cherry Pie

Yield: 8 servings

Sour cherries are available for only three to four weeks a year before the birds get to them. This is precisely what to do with those delish cherries. If you don't have a cherry/olive pitter, get one!

Position a rack in the lower third of the oven and line the floor of the oven with crumpled heavy-duty aluminum foil to catch any drippings. Preheat the oven to 425°F.

Combine the cherries, sugar, tapioca, water, lemon juice, and vanilla in a roomy bowl and let them stand for 15 minutes.

Line a 9-inch pie pan with 1 crust. Pour the cherry mixture into the bottom crust. Dot the mixture with the butter bits. Brush the overhanging edge of the crust with cold water. Cover with the top crust and seal the edge by crimping with a fork. Cut steam vents in the top crust. Beat the egg yolk and milk together with a fork, and brush the crust with the mixture. Bake the pie for 30 minutes.

If the edges of the pie crust are browning too rapidly, protect them either with a foil ring or a pie-crust shield. Reduce the oven temperature to 350°F and bake the pie for 25 to 35 minutes more until thick juices bubble through the vents. Let cool completely on a rack before cutting and serving.

5 cups pitted sour cherries (2 to 2½ pounds)

1 cup sugar

3 to 3½ tablespoons quick-cooking tapioca

2 tablespoons water

1 tablespoon strained fresh lemon juice

½ teaspoon vanilla extract

Purchased prepared pie crusts

3 tablespoons chilled, unsalted butter, cut into small pieces

1 large egg yolk

1 tablespoon whole milk or cream

Butterscotch Pie

Yield: one 9- to 10-inch pie

This rich and wonderful recipe is from the grandmother of a Midwestern family I know.

1½ cups packed brown sugar

2 tablespoons unsalted butter

1 cup water

Pinch of baking soda

3 large eggs yolks

¾ cup whole milk

2 tablespoons all-purpose flour

2 tablespoons cornstarch

1 teaspoon vanilla extract

Pinch of salt

1 blind-baked pie crust (9 to 10 inches)

In a saucepan, bring the brown sugar, butter, water, and baking soda to a boil, and simmer for 5 minutes. Keep warm.

Meanwhile, in a 1-quart Pyrex glass measure, whisk the egg yolks until pale yellow. In a heavy-bottomed sauce pan, bring the milk, flour, and cornstarch almost to a boil. Temper the egg yolks by adding ¼ cup of the hot milk mixture, whisking constantly, then add another ¼ cup, then the remaining hot milk.

Add the milk-egg mixture to the brown sugar–butter mixture. Whisk in the vanilla and salt.

Pour the mixture into the baked pie shell and refrigerate, at least 2 hours.

Moist Sugar Cake

Yield: one 13 x 9 x 2-inch cake

At first blush, this seems like a simple sugar cake. But something about the blend of ingredients turns out something absolutely irresistible. Be amply prepared to serve seconds of this lovely cake.

Preheat the oven to 350°F. Grease a 13 × 9 × 2-inch baking pan or dish (Pyrex is fine).

In a large bowl, whisk together the sifted flour, baking powder, baking soda, and salt.

In a stand blender, cream the butter with the cream cheese, 1¼ cups of sugar, the eggs, and vanilla. Add the flour mixture, alternating with the ½ cup of milk, a little at a time. Pour the batter into the prepared pan or dish.

For the topping: In the same stand blender, mix the 4 tablespoons of butter, ½ cup flour, and ½ cup sugar to crumbles.

Sprinkle the crumbs over the top of the cake, and bake for 30 to 40 minutes. Cool before serving.

2 cups sifted all-purpose flour

2 teaspoons baking powder

½ teaspoon baking soda

½ teaspoon salt

8 tablespoons (1 stick) unsalted butter, at room temperature

8 ounces cream cheese, at room temperature

1¼ cups sugar

2 large eggs

2 teaspoons vanilla extract

½ cup whole milk

CRUMB TOPPING
4 tablespoons (½ stick) unsalted butter

½ cup all-purpose flour

½ cup sugar

Rich Carrot Cake

Yield: one 13 x 9 x 2-inch cake

I make this lovely cake when I find I have too many carrots in the crisper drawer of my refrigerator.

¾ cup granulated sugar

1 cup packed brown sugar

1 cup corn oil

2 teaspoons vanilla extract

4 large eggs

2 cups all-purpose flour

1 teaspoon baking soda

1 teaspoon baking powder

1 teaspoon ground cinnamon

1 teaspoon ground allspice

1 teaspoon kosher salt

3 cups finely shredded carrots

Softened butter and flour, for the baking pan

FROSTING

8 ounces cream cheese, softened

4 tablespoons (½ stick) unsalted butter, softened

¾ cup confectioners' sugar

1 teaspoon vanilla extract

½ teaspoon salt

Preheat the oven to 350°F. Grease 13 × 9 × 2-inch baking pan or dish with butter and flour lightly.

Using a wooden spoon, or (better) an electric hand mixer, or a food processor, beat (or pulse) the sugars, oil, vanilla, and eggs together. Stir in the dry ingredients. Mix in carrots. Pour the batter into the prepared pan or dish and bake for 50 to 55 minutes. Let cool.

In a medium bowl, using an electric hand mixer, blend the cream cheese, butter, confectioners' sugar, vanilla, and salt together until creamy. Spread on the cooled cake.

To-Die-For Cheesecake

Yield: 1 delicious cheesecake, serves 8

I sometimes leave out the lemon zest in this incredibly luscious recipe, to let the vanilla and sugared cream cheese speak for themselves.

Preheat the oven to 500°F. Brush the sides and bottom of a 9-inch springform pan with the melted butter. Sprinkle graham cracker crumbs over the bottom of the pan and tilt it to coat evenly with the crumbs.

Beat the cream cheese in a stand mixer with the whisk attachment or wire beaters until very smooth. Gradually add the sugar and beat on medium speed until the sugar dissolves, about 3 minutes. Add the eggs, one at a time, beating just until incorporated and scraping down the sides of the mixer bowl after each addition. Add the lemon zest and vanilla and beat just until incorporated. Remove the bowl from the mixer and stir in cream and sour cream with a wooden spoon. Pour the batter into the prepared pan.

Bake the cheesecake at 500°F for 10 minutes. Reduce the oven temperature to 200°F and leave the oven door open until the temperature has reduced, 4 to 5 minutes. Bake until the cheesecake's perimeter is set, but the center jiggles when the pan is tapped, about 1 hour. Turn off the heat and, using a long-handled fork or spoon, prop open the oven door by about 1 foot. Let the cheesecake rest in the oven for 1 hour, then transfer it to a wire rack and let it cool to room temperature. Cover the cheesecake and refrigerate it until chilled, at least 4 hours.

1 tablespoon unsalted butter, melted

3 tablespoons graham cracker crumbs

2 pounds cream cheese (four 8-ounce bricks), at room temperature

1 cup superfine sugar

4 large eggs

1 teaspoon finely grated lemon zest

3 teaspoons vanilla extract

¼ cup heavy cream

¼ cup sour cream

Crème Brûlée

Yield: 4 servings

The blend of silky vanilla egg custard with a crunchy windowpane "brûlée" has an utterly addictive mouth-feel. It's fairly easy to do. Best made several hours ahead of time and hidden in the refrigerator, dessert is almost instantly ready when you are. Further, an opportunity is created to display the impressive flourish that only a blowtorch can provide. You'll need four 6-ounce heat- and flameproof ramekins.

Preheat the oven to 325°F. Heat the cream in a medium saucepan over medium heat until scalded; bubbles will form on the sides of the pan.

Using a sharp paring knife scrape the vanilla seeds from the pod, stir them into the hot cream, and let them steep for a few minutes. Or add the 1 teaspoon of vanilla extract.

In a medium bowl, gradually whisk the sugar into the egg yolks. Temper the yolks by slowly adding the hot cream into the yolk mixture, a few tablespoons at a time, whisking constantly.

Strain the mixture through a fine-mesh sieve into a 1-quart glass measuring cup with a pouring spout. Stir in the pinch of salt.

Arrange the ramekins in a deep baking pan roomy enough to accommodate them without touching. Pour the custard mixture into the ramekins. Transfer the pan to the oven shelf. Carefully fill the the pan with enough hot tap water to come halfway up the sides of the ramekins, then cover the entire pan tightly with heavy-duty aluminum foil.

(continued)

1 pint heavy cream

1 vanilla bean, split lengthwise (preferably) or 1 teaspoon vanilla extract

¼ cup sugar

5 large egg yolks

Pinch of kosher salt

1 to 2 tablespoons superfine sugar, for the topping brûlée

Bake until just set, 25 to 35 minutes. Be sure to start checking after 25 minutes; the baking time depends on the thickness and depth of the ramekins and baking pan. If you use glass ramekins, 25 minutes should do it. Ceramic ramekins may take 5 to 10 minutes longer. The custard should wobble like Jell-O, but not be soupy.

Put another way, when the custard moves as one mass rather than as a cup of liquid, it's ready. (If a knife or tester comes out clean, the custard has probably overcooked. Plunge the ramekins into shallow ice water immediately to prevent the custard from cooking any further.) Carefully remove from oven and let the ramekins cool, uncovered, in the water bath. Remove, cover each ramekin with plastic wrap, and refrigerate at least 2 hours.

Return the custards to room temperature before proceeding. Just before serving, preferably in full view of diner(s), sift a thin, even layer of sugar (superfine works best) over the custards, ignite a blowtorch according to the manufacturer's instructions, and with a slow, sweeping motion, guide the flame around the sugared surface of the custard. The nozzle should be 2 to 3 inches from the surface, with the tip of the flame licking the sugar. The sugar will melt slowly at first, then caramelize. As soon as the entire surface is a glossy mahogany color, move on to the next custard. Serve at once.

Flourless Chocolate Cake

Yield: 8 servings

This is just shamelessly rich, so a little will go a long way.

Preheat the oven to 375°F. Pour a bit of canola oil onto a folded paper towel, and rub a 9-inch springform pan with the oiled towel, then line the bottom with a circle of parchment paper. Rub the paper with canola oil, too, then set the pan aside.

Place 8 ounces of the chocolate and 1 cup (2 sticks) of the butter in a medium saucepan over medium-low heat. Melt the chocolate mixture, stirring often, until completely blended. Remove from the heat and transfer the mixture to a large bowl. Stir in the sugar and mix well. Add the eggs, one at a time, whisking well after each addition. Sift the cocoa into the bowl and stir until just blended.

Pour the batter into the prepared pan and bake for 35 to 40 minutes until the cake has risen and the top has formed a thin crust. The cake should be just barely firm in the center when it's done. Cool for 10 minutes, then invert onto a plate, removing the sides of the springform pan. Remove and discard the parchment paper and set the cake aside to cool completely.

Meanwhile, make the chocolate glaze. Melt the remaining 4 ounces of chocolate and 3 tablespoons of butter in a small saucepan over medium-low heat, stirring until smooth. Remove from the heat, then stir in the milk and vanilla. Set aside to cool slightly.

When the cake has cooled, pour the glaze onto the center. Using a spatula or the back of a spoon, very gently smooth the glaze along the top and sides of the cake.

Chill the cake, uncovered, for 30 to 60 minutes before serving to set the glaze and make the cake easier to slice.

Canola oil, for greasing the pan

12 ounces bittersweet chocolate, roughly chopped

1 cup (2 sticks) plus 3 tablespoons unsalted butter, cut into chunks

1 cup sugar

6 large eggs

1 cup good-quality unsweetened cocoa powder, such as Ghirardelli

1 tablespoon whole milk

½ teaspoon vanilla extract

Molten Chocolate Tarts

Yield: usually 9 tarts

Legend has it that this recipe began life as a mistake. Allegedly, a line cook in the kitchen of Jean-Georges Vongerichten accidentally undercooked some chocolate tarts, but the result is now on menus all over the country. When you cut into the cakey crust with your spoon, the warm pudding-like center comes oozing out. This recipe may have started out as a mistake, but so did Roquefort cheese.

16 tablespoons (2 sticks) unsalted butter, plus a little, soft butter, for buttering the molds

8 ounces bittersweet chocolate, preferably Valrhona

4 large eggs

4 large egg yolks

½ cup sugar

4 teaspoons all-purpose flour, plus a little more for dusting

Butter and lightly flour nine ½-cup capacity tart molds, and tap out all the excess flour.

Cut up the butter and break up the chocolate. Place both in a 1-quart Pyrex measure. Set aside.

Using an electric hand mixer, combine the eggs, egg yolks, and sugar and beat until thick and light.

Cook the butter and chocolate in the microwave oven for 2 minutes and 10 seconds at 50 percent power. Stir the nearly melted chocolate with the butter until smooth. Pour into the egg mixture, then quickly beat in the flour, just until combined.

Divide the batter among the molds. (At this point you can refrigerate the desserts until you are ready to eat, or for up to several hours. Bring them back to room temperature before cooking.)

Preheat the oven to 450°F. Place the molds on a baking sheet and bake for 6 to 7 minutes; the centers will still be quite soft, but the sides will be set.

Invert each mold onto a place and let sit for about 10 seconds. Unmold by lifting up one corner of the mold; the cake will fall out onto the plate. Serve immediately.

Intense Lemon Sorbet

Yield: about ⅔ quart sorbet

Not for sissies.

Blend the lemon juice, zest, water, sugar, and vodka in a large, non-reactive bowl. Stir until the sugar dissolves completely. Refrigerate the mixture, covered, until thoroughly chilled, at least 45 minutes.

Churn the mixture in an ice-cream machine according to the manufacturer's instructions until frozen, 20 to 30 minutes. Scoop the sorbet into a freezable container, and freeze it for at least 2 hours.

The sorbet keeps well for 3 to 4 days; then it usually hardens considerably.

1 cup freshly squeezed lemon juice (about 6 lemons)

Finely grated zest of 3 lemons

1 cup cold water

1 cup (or a bit less) of superfine sugar

1 tablespoon frozen vodka

Sitting on their terrace overlooking the Pacific Ocean, sharing Lemon Sorbet, Lennie turned to Lucky and said—"What's your definition of love?"

"Okay then," Lucky said, her dark eyes sparkling. "Falling in love with you was like getting hit by a truck yet not being mortally wounded. High one moment, low the next. Starving hungry, but unable to eat. And loving life with a mad passionate intensity. How about you?"

"Ah," Lennie said. "Loving you was inevitable. A crazy heartstopping rollercoaster ride. And even today I cannot wipe the smile off my face."

"And that's exactly the way it should be," Lucky said with a satisfied smile.

Crème Fraîche with Chocolate Mousse

Yield: 6 servings

The tanginess of the crème fraîche is soothed by the rich and creamy chocolate mousse, which is in turn lightened by the crème fraîche. This recipe uses uncooked egg whites and yolks. Small children or people with compromised immune systems should try another recipe.

In a saucepan over very low heat, melt the chocolate and the butter together. Just before the chocolate finishes melting, remove it from the heat and beat it with a whisk until smooth.

Transfer the chocolate mixture to a bowl and beat in the egg yolks with the whisk. Refrigerate.

Beat the egg whites with 2 tablespoons of the sugar until the whites hold stiff peaks but are not dry. Set aside. Beat the cream with the remaining 2 tablespoons sugar and the vanilla until it holds soft peaks.

Stir a couple of spoonfuls of the whipped whites into the chocolate mixture to lighten it, then fold in the remaining whites thoroughly but gently. Fold in the cream and refrigerate the mousse until chilled. If you are in a hurry, divide the mousse mixture among six cups; it will chill much faster. Serve the mousse within a day or two of making, under a generous scoop of crème fraîche.

2 tablespoons unsalted butter

4 ounces bittersweet or semisweet chocolate, chopped

3 large eggs, separated

¼ cup sugar

½ cup heavy cream

½ teaspoon vanilla extract

1 pint crème fraîche

Buttermilk Panna Cotta with Strawberries

Yield: 11 or 12 servings

Lunge for this recipe whenever local strawberries are in full-tilt season. You'll need a dozen 4-ounce Styrofoam cups to make this dessert. Always be extra careful when working with scalding hot caramelized sugar.

CARAMEL

1¼ cups sugar

Juice of ½ lemon

¼ cup water

PANNA COTTA

1 envelope gelatin (about 1 tablespoon)

¼ cup cold water

3 cups heavy cream

11 ounces sugar (1¼ cups plus 2 tablespoons)

1 cup buttermilk

Juice of 2 lemons, or to taste

2 to 3 dozen strawberries, washed and stemmed, halved, if you like

For the caramel: Combine the sugar and lemon juice in a small, heavy-bottomed pot. Add just enough water to moisten to a sandy texture. Brush any residual sugar off the sides of the pot with a pastry brush dipped in water. Cook over medium-high heat until the sugar caramelizes. Remove from heat and, standing at arm's length from the pot, add the ¼ cup water. Be careful: the mixture will bubble and sputter furiously. When the sputtering stops, carefully pour the caramel into eleven or twelve 4-ounce Styrofoam cups. Gently tilt the cups to coat with the caramel.

For the panna cotta: Soak the gelatin granules in ¼ cup cold water for 15 minutes, until softened.

Pour the cream into a saucepan and whisk in the sugar. Heat to just below a boil. Add the softened gelatin and stir until it dissolves completely. Stir in the buttermilk and lemon juice. Remove from heat and let cool.

Pour the custard into the caramelized molds. Refrigerate overnight, until the gelatin sets and the custards are stiff enough to unmold.

To unmold the custard, slip a small, sharp paring knife around the inside of the molds to loosen. Invert each cup over an individual serving plate and puncture the bottom (now the top) with the tip of the knife. Gently slide the panna cotta out of the cup.

Garnish with the strawberries.

Coconut Sorbet

Yield: 1 quart sorbet

I've tried to make coconut sorbet using fresh or canned plain coconut milk, but the results always seem to taste soapy. Coco Lopez to the rescue!

Two 15-ounce cans sweetened cream of coconut

2 cups ice water, minus the cubes

1 teaspoon plain vodka

Toasted sweetened coconut flakes, for serving

Whisk the cream of coconut, water, and vodka in a large glass measure. Transfer to a 12 × 8 × 2-inch glass baking dish. Freeze for about 3 hours, stirring every 30 minutes. Or freeze overnight, covered, stirring every 30 minutes for the first 3 hours.

Freeze the mixture in an ice-cream machine according to the manufacturer's instructions. Serve sprinkled with toasted coconut flakes

Max's favorite—including the vodka!

Index

Adele, 51

Amazing Caesar Salad, 20, *21*

ambiance, 51

Angel Hair Pasta with Sweet Sausage, Saffron, and
Cream, 43

Anthony, Marc, 30

appetizer(s), 18–19, 36–37

    angel hair with sausage, saffron, and cream, 43

    fettuccine with clams and chorizo, 48, *49*

    fettuccine with crab and cream, 47

    lasagne with mushrooms, sausage, cheese, and
prosciutto, 44–45

    linguine, lemon, 38

    macaroni and cheese, 29

    pasta puttanesca, 42

    penne alla vodka with tomatoes, sausage, bacon,
and cream, 40–41

    pizza, duck, with hoisin sauce, 30

    pizza, mushroom and sausage, 31

    pizza, pesto, *32, 33*

    pizza, salmon, 34

    rigatoni with bacon and mushrooms, 39

    rigatoni with lobster champagne cream, 50

    salad, beet and avocado, *22, 23*

    salad, Caesar, 20, *21*

    salad, orange and onion, *24, 25*

    sauce, veal, for, 46

    tapas, chorizo-chocolate, *26, 27*

    tart, mushroom and Gruyère, 28

Apple Crumble, 137

Baked Peaches with Cointreau, *134, 135*

Barbecue "Gonzalez" Sauce, 129

beef

    burgers, *82, 83*

    chili, 86, 87

    entrées, 78–94, *79, 82, 87, 92,* 102

    roast, *92, 93*

    Stroganoff, 84

Beef Tenderloin Steaks with Brandy and Mustard
Sauce, 90

The Best Hamburger in Town!, *82, 83*

The Best Mashed Potatoes Ever!, 108

Blender Hollandaise Sauce, 83, 131

Blue Cheese and Caramelized Onion Potatoes au
Gratin, 124

Bobby and Denver's White Wine Sangria, 14

Bourbon Chicken Milanese, 63

Bourbon-Marinated Flank Steak, 94

Breaking Bad, 47

Brussels Sprouts Moutarde, *120, 121*

burgers

    beef, *82, 83*

    duck, 71

Buttermilk Panna Cotta with Strawberries, 152, *153*

Butterscotch Pie, 140

Caipirinhas Cocktail, 10

cake. *See also* dessert

    carrot, 142

    cheese-, 143

    flourless chocolate, 147

    sugar, 141

caramel sauce, 152

Cheesy Cauliflower Gratin, 123

chicken

    bourbon Milanese, 63

    breasts with fontina and prosciutto, 59

breasts with lemons, olives, and capers, *66, 67*

cacciatore, 62

drumsticks, 57

entrées, 57–69, *61, 66*

fried, 58

lime, with fontina and chile, 64–65

paella with chorizo, 60–61, *61*

Chicken Breasts with Fontina and Prosciutto, 59

Chicken Breasts with Roasted Lemons, Green
       Olives, and Capers, *66, 67*

Chicken Cacciatore, 62

Chicken Paella with Spanish Chorizo, 60–61, *61*

chili

beef, 86, *87*

sauce, 64

Chorizo-Chocolate Tapas, *26, 27*

cocktail(s), 4–5

Bellini, 8–9, 65

Bloody Mary, 13

caipirinhas, 10

The Jackie Collins, *6, 7*

Manhattan, 12, *12*

margarita, 11, *11*

martini, lychee, 16, *17*

Midori sour, 15

sangria, 14

wassail, 15

Coconut Sorbet, 154

Coq au Vin, 68–69

Crabby Portobello Mushrooms, 125

Cranberry-Orange Chutney, 128

Creamed Fresh Corn-Stuffed Red Bell Peppers,
       115–16, *117*

Creamy Macaroni and Cheese, 29

Creamy Peas with Tarragon, 112, *112*

Crème Brûlée, *144,* 145–46

Crème Fraîche with Chocolate Mousse, *150,* 151

crumb toppings, 137, 141

dessert, 132–33

cake, carrot, 142

cake, cheese-, 143

cake, flourless chocolate, 147

cake, sugar, 141

crème brûlée, *144,* 145–46

crème fraîche with mousse, *150,* 151

crumble, apple, 137

panna cotta with strawberries, 152, *153*

peaches, baked, with Cointreau, *134,* 135

pie, butterscotch, 140

pie, cherry, 139

pie, pear and blueberry with oatmeal crust, 138

sorbet, coconut, 154

sorbet, lemon, 149

tart, molten chocolate, 148

tart, pear, 136

Deviled Chicken Drumsticks, 57

Drake, 57

Dried Chile Sauce, 64

duck, 71

pizza, 30

Duck Burgers with Onion Marmalade, 71

Eggplant Parmesan, 56

English Roast Potatoes, 109

entrees

beef burgers, *82, 83*

beef chili, 86, *87*

beef flank steak with bourbon, 94

beef meatballs, 80–81

beef meat loaf, 88–89

beef, roast, with coriander, *92, 93*

beef steak tartare, 91

beef Stroganoff, 84

beef tenderloin steaks with brandy and mustard,
      90

chicken breasts with fontina and prosciutto, 59

chicken breasts with lemons, olives, and capers, 66, 67
chicken cacciatore, 62
chicken drumsticks, deviled, 57
chicken, fried, 58
chicken, lime, with fontina and dried chile, 64–65
chicken Milanese, bourbon, 63
chicken paella with chorizo, 60–61, 61
chicken with wine, 68–69
duck burgers with onion marmalade, 71
eggplant Parmesan, 56
lamb, baked, 96
lamb steak with mushrooms, 95
pork chops Milanese, 73
pork chops saltimbocca with sautéed spinach, 74
pork tacos, pulled, 76, 77
pork tenderloin with honey-mustard, 75
salmon, miso, 100, 101
sausages with grapes, 70
shrimp in lemon-coconut milk, 98, 99
skate with lobster rice, 102
sole with Parmesan crust, 103
spareribs, sweet and spicy, 78, 79
turkey, baked, with mustard, 72
veal scallops with vegetables, 97
zucchini boats, 54, 55

Fettuccine with Clams and Chorizo, 48, 49
Fettuccine with Crab and Cream, 47
Flourless Chocolate Cake, 147
fondue, 118, 119
frosting, 142

Gaga, Lady, 33, 87
Gaye, Marvin, 11

Gino's Favorite Pesto Pizza, 32, 33
Gino the Ram's Special Spicy Bloody Marys, 13
glaze, plum, 129. See also marinade/rub; sauce(s)
The Godfather, 45
Green Beans with Cumin for a Crowd, 113
Grilled Lime Chicken with Fontina Cheese and Dried Chile Sauce, 64–65

Hazan, Marcella, 46
"Hero" (song), 11

Iglesias, Enrique, 11, 51
Intense Lemon Sorbet, 149

The Jackie Collins (cocktail), 6, 7
Jay-Z, 57

Kelly, R., 65
Kittichai Restaurant, New York City, 16

Lamb Steaks with Mushrooms, 95
Lamb You Can Eat with a Spoon, 96
Lasagne with Wild Mushrooms, Sausage, Four Cheeses, and Prosciutto, 44–45
Lemon Linguine, 38
Lennie Has a Yen for the Definitive Manhattan (cocktail), 12, 12
Levine, Adam, 87
lobster
    champagne cream, 50
    rice, 102
Lucky's Best Besciamella Sauce, 130
Lucky's Get-You-Going-Turkey, 72
Lucky's Kick-Ass Chili, 86, 87

Lucky's Killer Margaritas, 11, *11*
Lucky's Luscious Meatballs, 80–81
Lucky's Special Southern Fried Chicken, 58

Mandarin Orange and Red Onion Salad, 24, *25*
marinade/rub. *See also* sauce(s)
    bourbon, 63, 94
    lime, 64–65
    mustard, 72
    plum glaze and, 129
marmalade, onion, 71
Martin, Dean, 34
Martin, Ricky, 30
Max's Beet and Avocado Salad, 22, *23*
meatballs, 80–81
meat loaf, 88–89
Midori Sours, 15
Moist Sugar Cake, 141
Molten Chocolate Tarts, 148
mood, setting of, 51
Mushroom and Gruyère Tart, 28

New Potato Salad, 106

panna cotta, 152, *153*
pasta. *See also* appetizer(s)
    angel hair with sausage, saffron, and cream, 43
    as appetizers, 29, 37–50
    as entrée, 84
    fettuccine with clams and chorizo, 48, *49*
    fettuccine with crab and cream, 47
    lasagne with mushrooms, sausage, cheese, and
        prosciutto, 44–45
    linguine, lemon, 38
    macaroni and cheese, 29

penne alla vodka with tomatoes, sausage, bacon,
    and cream, 40–41
    puttanesca, 42
    rigatoni with bacon and mushrooms, 39
    rigatoni with lobster champagne cream, 50
    sauce, veal saffron cream, 46
    seafood, 47–50, *49*
Pasta Puttanesca, 42
Pear and Blueberry Pie with Buttery Oatmeal
    Crust, 138
Pear Tart, 136
Penne alla Vodka Martini with Tomatoes, Sausage,
    Bacon, and Cream, 40–41
Peppered Beef Stroganoff, 84
Perfect Cherry Pie, 139
pie. *See also* dessert
    butterscotch, 140
    cherry, 139
    pear and blueberry, 138
Pitbull, 33
pizza
    duck, smoked, 30
    mushroom and sausage, 31
    pesto, *32*, 33
    salmon, smoked, 34
Pizza with Mushroom and Sausage, 31
Plum Glaze, 129
pork, 106
    appetizers, 26, 31, 39–41, 43–45, 48, *49*
    entrées, *54*, 55, 70, 73–78, *76*, 79, 115–16, *117*
    pastas, 43–45, 48, *49*
    on pizza, 31
    side dishes with, 115–16, *117*
Pork Chops Milanese, 73
Pork Chops Saltimbocca with Sautéed Spinach, 74
Pork Tenderloin with Honey-Mustard Sauce, 75
potato(es)
    au gratin, 124
    balls, 107, *107*

mashed, 108

roasted, 109

salad, 106

sweet, 111

Potato Balls Sautéed in Butter, 107, *107*

poultry

chicken, 57–69, *61, 66*

turkey, 72

Puck, Wolfgang, 7, *7*

Pulled Pork Tacos, *76,* 77

rice

lobster, 102

paella, 60–61, *61*

in shrimp stew, 98

in stuffed peppers, 115–16

in zucchini boats, *54, 55*

Rich Carrot Cake, 142

Rigatoni with Bacon and Shiitake Mushrooms, 39

Rigatoni with Lobster Champagne Cream, 50

Roast Beef Dusted with Coriander, *92, 93*

Roasted Broccoli with Fondue, 118, *119*

Roasted Butternut Squash, 110

Roasted Sage Sausages and Grapes, 70

Roasted Veal Scallops with Vegetables, 97

Rococo Meat loaf, 88–89

Sade, 15, 51

sake butter, 101

salad(s)

as appetizers, 20–25, *21–22, 24*

with beet and avocado, *22, 23*

Caesar, 20, *21*

with oranges and onions, *24,* 25

potato, 106

as side dish, 106

salmon

with miso, *100,* 101

pizza, 34

Santangelo Salmon, *100, 101*

sauce(s), 126–27

barbecue, 78, 129

besciamella, 130

brandy and mustard, 90

caramel, 152

chili, dried, 64

chutney, cranberry-orange, 128

hollandaise, 83, 131

honey mustard, 75

marinades and, 63, 64–65, 72, 94

marmalade, onion, 71

miso, 101

plum, 129

puttanesca, 42

veal saffron cream, 46

seafood

appetizers, 34, 47–50, *49*

clam, 48, *49*

crab, 47, 125

entrees, 98–103, *99–100*

lobster, 50, 102

pastas, 47–50, *49*

salmon, 34, *100, 101*

shrimp, 98, *99*

side dishes with, 125

sole, 103

stew, 98, *99*

seasoned stock, 80

Shrimp in Lemony Coconut Milk, 98, *99*

side dish(es), 104–5, *122*

of bell peppers, corn-stuffed, 115–16, *117*

of broccoli, roasted, with fondue, 118, *119*

of Brussels sprouts with mustard, *120,* 121

of cauliflower gratin, 123

of crab with portobello mushrooms, 125

of green beans, slow-braised, 114

of green beans with cumin, 113
of peas with tarragon, 112, *112*
of potato balls, sautéed, 107, *107*
of potatoes au gratin with blue cheese and
    onion, 124
of potatoes, mashed, 108
of potatoes, roasted, 109
of potato salad, 106
of squash, roasted butternut, 110
of sweet potatoes with apricot, 111
Sinatra, Frank, 34
Skate with Lobster Rice, 102
Slow-Braised Green Beans, 114
Smoked Duck Pizza with Hoisin Sauce, 30
Smoked Salmon Pizza, 34
"Smooth Operator" (song), 15
Sole with Parmesan Crust, 103
sorbet
  coconut, 154
  lemon, 148
Steak Tartare, 91
Steines, Mark, 7
stew, seafood, 98, 99
Sweet and Spicy Spareribs, 78, 79
Sweet Potatoes and Apricots, 111

table setting, 51
tart(s). *See also* dessert
  as appetizer, 28
  chocolate, 148
  as desserts, 136, 148
  mushroom and Gruyère, 28
  pear, 136
To-Die-For Cheesecake, 143
turkey entrees, 72

Usher, 51

veal, 73, 74
  pasta, 46
  scallops, 97
Veal Saffron Cream Pasta Sauce, 46
The Venus Bellini, 8–9, 65
The Venus Lychee Martini, 16, *17*
Vongerichten, Jean-Georges, 148

Wassail, 15
"What's Going On" (song), 11
Winehouse, Amy, 15

Zucchini Boats, *54, 55*